PHILOSOPHICAL PROPOSITIONS

PHILOSOPHICAL PROPOSITIONS

An Introduction to Philosophy

Jonathan Westphal

London and New York

First published 1998
by Routledge
11 New Fetter Lane, London EC4P 4EE

Simultaneously published in the USA and Canada
by Routledge
29 West 35th Street, New York, NY 10001

Typeset in Aldus Roman by RefineCatch Limited, Bungay, Suffolk
Printed and bound in Great Britain by Clays Ltd, St Ives, PLC

British Library Cataloging in Publication Data
A catalogue record for this book is available from the British Library

Library of Congress Cataloguing in Publication Data
Westphal, Jonathan
Philosophical propositions: an introduction to philosophy /
Jonathan Westphal.
Includes index.
ISBN 0–415–17052–4. — ISBN 0–415–17053–2 (pbk.)
1. Philosophy—Introductions.   2. Analysis (Philosophy)
I. Title.
BD21.W44   1998
100 – dc21   97–33483

ISBN 0–415–17052–4 (hbk)
ISBN 0–415–17053–2 (pbk)

The scapegoat, on which one lays one's sins, and who runs away into the desert with them – a false picture, similar to those that cause errors in philosophy.

Wittgenstein, 'Philosophy'

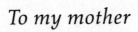

To my mother

Contents

Figures

Preface

This introduction to philosophy takes the view that solutions to the problems of philosophy depend on philosophical analysis. Analysis has been astonishingly fruitful in twentieth-century philosophy, and it has taken many forms. In this book I take it, very broadly, to mean replacing a problematic proposition with an unproblematic proposition which as nearly as possible says the same thing, or replacing a problematic formulation of a proposition by an unproblematic formulation of the same proposition. This is a pretty rough-and-ready characterization of philosophical analysis, but what philosophical analysis is – the precise analysis of the phrase 'philosophical analysis' – is itself a delicate and advanced philosophical topic. The theme of the book is that we know enough about how analysis works to use it to cut our way through the thickets of philosophy. One does not always need to be able to say or even to know exactly what something is in order to be able to use it effectively.

The book has been written as a textbook for an Introduction to Philosophy class, covering one American college semester. Its introductory purpose has not stopped me from arguing for definite views of my own, some of them very much minority views. In Chapter 8, for example, I urge the merits of neutral monism, a theory whose last champion was A.J. Ayer in *Language, Truth and Logic*, published in 1936.

I hope that the book will be useful to those wanting or needing to learn about philosophy, and also that it will be of interest to those who already know the subject.

Jonathan Westphal
Idaho
March 1997

Acknowledgements

I wish to thank my colleagues in the Philosophy Program at Idaho State University for much valuable discussion and criticism, especially Russell Wahl and Bill King. It is the students in Philosophy 151 at Idaho State University (now Philosophy 101, Introduction to Western Thought) who have contributed most to the book, however. To them I can say that they deserve the book, as well as my thanks. I also wish to thank the Routledge readers and editors for their advice and suggestions. I am most grateful to Clive Swansbourne for catching several big mistakes in the arguments, and to Deborah Wilkes of Hackett Publishing for encouragement and advice in the book's development.

1
The Nature of a Philosophical Problem
What Is Philosophy?

A
Introduction

Many introductions to philosophy do not define their subject matter. The best introduction to philosophy, some of them say, is philosophy itself, and the best way to learn what philosophy is is to get on and do some.

This bracing answer to the question presupposes that one already knows what it is that one is supposed to be getting on with. 'Doing philosophy' can simply amount to following erratically in the footsteps of the philosophical writer one happens to be reading.

Someone who genuinely has no idea at all what philosophy is, and wishes to know, surely deserves a genuine answer. Even some professional philosophers are in this deserving category. These philosophers have not come to a settled view of what their subject is, and they may be ashamed to confess it.

Or they may confess it freely. 'What philosophy is is itself a philosophical question', they say. This is of course true, but it is not the end of the matter, for even so, it ought to be possible to say what philosophy is as one understands it.

It has been said[1] that in philosophy 'the difficulties and disagreements of which its history is full, are mainly due to a very simple cause: namely to the attempt to answer questions, without first discovering precisely *what* question it is which you desire to answer'. This is certainly part of the problem.

In what follows, a proposition or statement at the centre of a philosophical problem or problems, a 'problem proposition' as I will call it, will be given, and the downward arrow '↓' used to mark the transformation of this problem proposition into one which does not raise the problem or problems, or to mark another proposition which replaces it and which does not raise the problem or problems. This has traditionally been called an 'analysis'. The downward arrow will signify that the original proposition and the analysed proposition are equivalent, and it will also indicate the direction of the analysis, from the initial proposition to the analysed proposition.

Philosophical analyses can, however, not only fail to solve given specified problems. They can also generate new problems of their own.

I shall use the phrase 'philosophical problem' to refer narrowly to the kind of puzzle which a philosophical analysis resolves. But I shall also use this phrase in a wider way to refer to any large-scale intellectual problem whose solution depends on philosophical analysis. In this second sense a philosophical problem consists of a philosophical question and the attempt to answer it by means of a rational argument. It might be better to reserve the phrase 'philosophical puzzle' for a philosophical problem in the first and narrower sense. Or one could say that there are two kinds of philosophical problem. There is the chaotic and chronologically prior kind which consists of wonder and confusion, and there is the clear and logically prior kind which consists of organized puzzlement and resolution.

B
What Philosophy Is

As I propose to define it, philosophy is the attempt, by means of rational argument, to resolve those problems, typically of great practical importance or theoretical interest, which depend on the analysis of the basic concepts in the propositions in which they are stated. So the central activity of philosophy in this sense is analysis.

Consider the difference between two questions about time. The first one, 'What is the time?' or 'What time is it?', is answered by giving a number which marks a place on a fixed scale of hours, minutes and seconds. This point is determined by looking at a watch, or listening to the speaking clock, or following the sun in the sky. The second question, 'What is time?', cannot be answered by any of these empirical activities. What is at issue in the second question is not where on the fixed scale the present is to be found, but the nature of what the scale scales. G.E. Moore said that though he did not know what time is, finding it philosophically a very puzzling thing indeed, he *did* know that he had had his breakfast before his lunch.

The philosopher Rudolf Carnap generalized this point by distinguishing what he called 'internal' from 'external' questions.[2] 'What time is it?' is a question which can be answered *within* or using the scheme of concepts which includes the concept *time*. The second question, what time is, asks about the interpretation and application of the scheme of concepts itself, and it is 'external' to the scheme in Carnap's sense. The second question demands an analysis of the concept, not an unanalysed application of it.

Or suppose that there is a question about what we *see*. Someone might answer the question simply by listing the objects in his or her field of vision. That would be an internal answer to the question. Taking the question externally, one might wonder about what *seeing* is, about whether one is ever really in direct contact with the objects which appear to be in the field of vision, or whether one is really only in contact with one's own perceptions.

Or finally, to take one of Carnap's own examples, the question of whether there is a prime number lying beyond one hundred is an internal question. The question of whether there are *any numbers at all*, as opposed to things like horses and men, and people counting them, is an external question, and it is a philosophical question. It concerns the whole category or concept of number.

Philosophy undertaken as analysis can, however, play a critical role even in the empirical sciences, for example in physical cosmology. Take the question of how the existence of the universe is to be explained, if it can be. Why does the universe exist? Some physicists have tried to give an account of how the universe arose out of nothing. It turns out, however, that their 'nothing' is actually a rather definite sort of something, namely a something which they describe as fluctuations in a sea of quantum gravity. So 'The universe arose out of nothing' is being given a very special sense, one in which 'nothing' also means 'something'. Here a conception of the world hinges on a concept which cries out for philosophical analysis.

Philosophy also has a special role in the understanding of religion. Consider a classic problem about the creation of the world. There is a reason for everything, suppose. So there is a reason for the world. This reason cannot lie within the world, for then it would be a part of the world and not a reason for it. So it lies outside the world. It transcends the world. Call this transcendent reason or 'creator' God. But then what is the reason for God? Who or what created God? Or is there an infinite hierarchy of ascending 'supergods', as they might be called?

This is a question regularly asked by even quite small children. The answer involves an analysis or an understanding of what is meant by 'reason', 'create', 'world' and so on, which are the key concepts in the problem.

What is at issue in both the physics of cosmology and the theology of creation is the understanding of *concepts*, not just the discovery of new facts. Indeed, an uncritical and wholly factual way of thinking is in part responsible for the cosmological and theological problems. The problems are conceptual, not just factual.

I also very much respect the view that philosophy is the attempt to arrive at coherent, overall pictures of the world in which everything fits together nicely. On this view academic philosophy is the discussion which takes place when conceptions of the world, or basic beliefs, come into conflict with one another.

There is certainly much to be said for a view like this, though I think that it has more to do with a personal *motivation* for philosophy than it does with its public result. In practice, however, the view tends to turn into the view that philosophy is conceptual analysis. Pictures of the world are not all intrinsically philosophical; for example, the picture in which everything is made of little elastic balls, though this (Greek atomism) had its origin in metaphysics. Such views become philosophical only when their key terms are subjected to a philosophical or conceptual scrutiny driven by puzzles.

So we still need to know what a philosophical analysis is. What is meant by the phrase 'analysis of the basic concepts' in the definition of philosophy given above?

C
Two Model Problems of Philosophical Analysis

Consider the following propositions. I offer them as examples of propositions which embody philosophical problems and call for philosophical analysis.

The average American family has 2.6 children.

Why is this proposition a problem? Certainly it is true.

The Puzzle of the Average American Family
Yet how can it be? For there is no such thing as 'the average American family'. Even if there were, there would be no answer to the question of where this family lives, or what it is called. The general problem is how a proposition like the problem proposition can be true when its subject does not exist. The problematic concept here is *the average American family*.

The Puzzle of the Divided Children
Yet how can it be? For there is no such thing as 2.6 children. The general problem is how a proposition can be true and a predicate like '2.6 children' truly applied when the predicate does not refer to anything. The problematic concept here is *2.6 children*.

Reflecting on the initial proposition, one might try to distinguish between the world of reality and the world of statistics. This raises further questions.

What is a statistical child, if not a child?
How does a statistical child differ from a real child, if it does?
What is the relation between the two types of child?

There is no real doubt about what the given proposition means, however, and it is interesting that this meaning is given by the calculation which establishes the statistic. Nor is there much doubt about what it does not mean. It does not mean that in an average state, somewhere, out there, probably in Ohio, behind a white picket fence, just off Main Street, there really does exist the average American family. And it has one dog and 2.6 children.

Disappointing as it may seem to those enticed by this picture, the proposition actually means that the number of American children divided by the number of American families is 2.6.

So we have,

The average American family has 2.6 children.
↓
The number of American children divided by the number of American families is 2.6.

This final proposition immediately resolves the puzzle of the average American family and the puzzle of the divided children. In it the word 'average' has disappeared. Indeed, it could be regarded as giving a definition of the word 'average', which explains why the word appears in the original proposition but not in its analysis.

The phrase 'the average American family' in the first proposition has been broken up, and so the final proposition does not even seem to refer to something called 'the average American family'. 'Family' has been replaced by the plural 'families'. The grammatical subject of the second proposition is 'the number of American children divided by the number of American families', not 'the average American family'.

The phrase '2.6 children' has been broken up, so that the final proposition does not even seem to refer to a group of children, 2.6 in number. '2.6' no longer modifies 'children'. Instead, it flanks the equational verb in the final proposition. For what this proposition says is that a number, the number of American children, divided by another number, the number of American families, is a third number, 2.6. There is nothing problematic about the concept that a number divided by another number is a third number, whereas there clearly is in the idea of 2.6 children something very problematic indeed.

The final proposition also avoids the three problems about the relation of the real to the statistical children. These problems are creatures of the unanalysed original proposition, and when it is replaced they too disappear. In this sense, they find their resolution in the final proposition.

The main mistake which generates the puzzles is thinking that the logical form of 'The average American family has 2.6 children' is the same as the logical form of 'The First Family has 2 children.' The grammatical subject of the first is not its real subject, whereas the grammatical subject of the second is its real subject. It looks as though the proposition about the average American family is about the average American family, just as the proposition about the First Family is about the Clintons, but this appearance is misleading. The first proposition really says something about the number of American children divided by the number of American families, not about a particular family.

Something can now be said about the phrase 'basic concepts' in the final definition of philosophy given earlier. 'Basic concepts' can be understood to be those concepts which do or could yield a philosophical puzzle. Thus in the initial proposition about the average American family, by this test, the problematic basic concepts are 'average' and '2.6 children'.

'Has' and 'family' would not count as problematic basic concepts in connection with the puzzles associated with the initial proposition. But they could well be counted as problematic concepts in the intended sense in other problem propositions or in connection with other puzzles; for example, those raised by 'I *have* a pain.' Does 'have' here mean the same as in 'I *have* a question' or 'I *have* a cat'? Or what is a *family*? Do only nuclear families count? What if the parents of children 1 and 2 are divorced and marry the separated but unmarried biological parents of children 3 and 4? How many families are left? *None* (because the families have broken up); *one* (because it's all one big extended happy family); *two* (because the facts of parenthood and the relationships of the parents to the children have not changed); *three* (because there are two original families plus one new grouping); and *four* (two old and two new) – these are all more or less defensible answers. And then what if the parents of children 1 and 2 are not their biological parents, but have adopted them, and are also themselves gay? Does a family based on a gay marriage count as a family? How about if it takes place in church? (How about if it doesn't?) So here the concept *families* is beginning to look problematic, and there are serious philosophical questions involved in how to identify them and how to count them.

Consider another problem proposition.

Nothing is perfect.

Many people believe that this proposition is true. On reflection, some of them might imagine nothing as a large, quiet and frightening patch of nullity, rather like a fog. They might also imagine that it is perfect in its uncanny silence and its white purity. They would then be bound to understand the proposition to mean that there is something called 'Nothing', and that it is Perfect. This Nothing might also be blamed for the various phenomena of negativity in the world, including absences, illnesses and the like. (Then what of its perfectness? Perhaps it is jealous of the perfection of other things.) Such an analysis might even be thought to have theological implications.

The philosophical interest of the proposition therefore lies as much in its meanings – it surely has several! – as in its truth.

> The Puzzle of the Existence of Nothing
> The proposition appears to be about nothing, in the sense that its grammatical subject is 'nothing'. Yet if it is about nothing, how can it be true? And if it is true, and it is about nothing, then there is after all something – nothing – which it is about. Then nothing is after all something. And so on.

> The Puzzle of the Perfection of Nothing
> Even supposing that nothing is a sort of eerie void, but still a something, how can it be, as the proposition seems to say, *perfect*? Is it not instead maximally *imperfect*, having as it does no redeeming positive characteristics whatever?

These two problems are based on a misunderstanding of the function of 'nothing' or 'no thing'. The problematic concept in both puzzles is *nothing*. For what the proposition says, on its most natural reading, is that everything is imperfect.

We have,

Nothing is perfect.
↓
Everything is imperfect.

Getting this analysis involves first taking a universal negative type of proposition, and seeing that 'nothing' means 'no thing'. Then it involves changing 'No thing is perfect' to 'Everything is imperfect.' This step uses the logical operation called *obversion*, by which 'X is not pure' becomes 'X is impure' and vice versa. Finally, the analysis can proceed further if 'Everything is imperfect' in turn is read as 'Pick anything you please, you will find that it is imperfect', in order to head off the problem that the final proposition might now seem to refer to a large entity called 'everything'.

The analysis short-circuits both the puzzle of the existence of nothing and the puzzle of the perfection of nothing, because its grammatical subject is not 'nothing', but 'everything', this to be taken further as 'anything' as in 'Pick anything you please.' This does not say of this anything you please, or of anything else, that it is perfect, but the opposite, that whatever anything is, it is imperfect.

D
Philosophical Problems and Pictures

The two model problems generated by the two given propositions in the previous section differ in several important respects from full-scale philosophical problems.

1 For one thing, they are less difficult to resolve.
2 They are also not of obvious practical importance or general theoretical interest. (Communist governments, though, would have benefited from philosophical analysis when thinking about their belief in the reality and virtues of the 'average man' depicted with socialist 'realism' on Soviet billboards. 'Average industrial man' was in fact a metaphysical abstraction!)
3 The conception of an analysis (represented above by '↓') which is needed to resolve them is relatively limited in scope. In c. 1930 propositions about averages were the standard example of a problem-proposition to be resolved by analysis, which consisted of an exact translation of an initial proposition into an analysed proposition. The resolution given of the second problem, the one about 'Nothing', is of a different type, based on the translation techniques of symbolic logic.
4 A fourth difference between the two model problems and live philosophical problems, which makes the model problems easier to solve, is that they do not arise in the context of an intellectually pressing question, whose answer is being sought by means of rational argument.

Analysis has taken the form of the attempt to give a general definition of an abstract concept, and also of the attempt to give alternative accounts of problematic notions such as those of *causation* and *material substance*, and other things as well. This raises the question as to which form of analysis is the correct one, and hence the further question as to what the correct general analysis is of the proposition 'Proposition A is the analysis of proposition P.' This is a delicate and advanced question. Analysis can, however, proceed quite successfully before it is necessary to decide the nature of analysis itself. All that is needed for the moment is the notion of an initial proposition being reformulated as, or replaced by, an analysed proposition, with the result that the puzzles are resolved.

The model philosophical problems appear when the understanding of the initial problem propositions is distorted by a picture which dominates our understanding of them. There is the picture of an average family, happily ensconced on Main Street, dog and all, and there is the picture of Nothing as an evanescent Something. These misleading pictures result from taking too seriously one or another apparent implication of the structure or content of the problem propositions. The first takes too seriously the fact that 'the average American family' is the grammatical subject of 'The average American family has 2.6 children' and perhaps the emotional force of 'average American'. The second takes too seriously the fact that 'nothing' is the apparent subject of the proposition, and 'perfect', rather than 'imperfect', its predicate. It takes too seriously the superficial or surface resemblance between 'Nothing is perfect' and 'Lucy is perfect.' Getting rid of these resemblances is the means by which the puzzles can be resolved, when an initial proposition is replaced by an analysis whose form does not generate a misleading or false picture or comparison.

What is *not* needed to resolve the puzzles is an abstract or theoretical solution, a factual theory. We do not need, for example, a theory which postulates the existence of an abstract perfect ideal type to solve the problems. Nor do we need to postulate the existence of Nothing, somehow in the mode of something, a something which is unique in that its mode of being is non-being. All that these solutions can do is to reflect the problems. In fact, they *are* the problems.

So in the two model problems we have:

Initial proposition → Analysed proposition: Resolution of puzzle
↓
False logical form
↓
False picture
↓
Puzzle
↓
Theoretical solution

By replacing the problem propositions with the analysed propositions, in which the real import of the problem propositions is given, the whole process from false pictures through puzzles to solutions is by-passed. Needed, in addition to the discovery of the all-important analysed proposition (which is a recognition of the falsity of the false logical form), are the ability to wrestle clear of the false picture, and the willingness to give up the security apparently offered by the abstract theoretical solution. These form perhaps the hardest but the most satisfying part of philosophy.

Some of the big questions of traditional philosophy, in this view, are puzzles which can be understood as a consequence of the false pictures we derive from the initial propositions, and from which the analysed propositions can free us. The first three stages, of question, argument and initial proposition, together form a *philosophical problem*. What happens when such problems are resolved is that formless or unclear problems are converted into puzzles, and then resolved by analysis.

What criteria govern the acceptability of a proposed analysis? There are several.

The analysis resolves the puzzles.

It clears up the false pictures which generate the puzzles. The puzzles can be resolved without any clarity resulting. It has been said of the philosopher Hume, for example, that he had a baffling genius for the destructive analysis of problems without resolving the underlying thought-forms or pictures which gave rise to them.

The analysed propositions must as far as possible say the same thing as the initial propositions. An exception to this condition can be made when the initial proposition is false or otherwise defective. Some philosophers have believed that propositions about minds, such as 'John's mind is made up', fit this category, and that they should be replaced by propositions about the neurophysiological activity in John's brain. The onus is on someone offering an analysis like this to give independent reasons for believing that the original proposition is indeed false or defective. In addition, some settled criteria must be given for assessing a constructive or 'replacement' analysis.

The previous condition raises the question of what criteria other than 'saying the same thing' govern 'replacement' analyses. 'Conformity to the scientific world-picture' is a criterion sometimes heard, but this seems on the same level as 'Conformity to the religious world-picture', as if there were such a thing. Some balance must be found between exact equivalence of initial and analysed propositions, rare outside model problems like the ones given, and the application of such criteria, or the question will arise of what justification can be given for saying that it is indeed the original, initial proposition, and not some other one, which has been analysed.

The older methods of philosophy give positive theories about the solutions to philosophical problems. The philosophical method of analysis, which halts the sequence from initial propositions to theoretical solutions, might seem *negative* by comparison. There is perhaps some truth to this criticism, but it also embodies a false form for a certain initial proposition, the proposition that 'Philosophical analysis produces only negative results', and a false picture of a negative result to go with it.

What, after all, is a *negative* result? Consider the proposition that 'Medical work only produces negative results.' It could be said that the efforts of doctors, nurses, medical technicians and those who devote themselves to medical research are *negative*, because their aim is the prevention and elimination of illness and disease. Good health itself is not a *positive*, detectable entity. This does not mean, however, that good health is non-existent, and it certainly does not mean that the efforts of the medical professions are any the less valuable, certainly not *just* because they have as their aim the prevention and elimination of something. For what is prevented and eliminated is supremely worth preventing and eliminating.

Historical Note

Early in the development of Western philosophy Socrates, the Greek philosopher for whom philosophy was an inquiry into how to live, began an inquiry into various abstract notions, such as *justice* and *knowledge*, by asking questions which typically took the form, 'What is justice?', 'What is knowledge?' and so on. Many of the works of Plato, the author of the celebrated philosphical dialogues, and with Aristotle one of the two really big figures in Ancient Greek philosophy, record the attempt to answer these questions. The analysis of material things as perceptions given by George Berkeley, the seventeeth-century Irish philosopher, is an example of an account in which a common notion is revised by an allegedly superior one. So is the negative analysis of causation as constant conjunction given by David Hume, the empiricist and sceptical philosopher, in the eighteenth century. The formal technique of replacing a problem-proposition with an analysis, traditionally called 'philosophical analysis', was the contribution of the twentieth-century Cambridge philosophers Bertrand Russell and G.E. Moore. It replaced an older and more haphazard metaphysical approach to philosophy. 'A logical theory may be tested by its capacity for dealing with puzzles, and it is a wholesome plan, in thinking about logic, to stock the mind with as many puzzles as possible, since these serve much the same purpose as is served by experiments in physical science', Russell wrote in 'On Denoting'.[3] In 'Systematically Misleading Expressions' Gilbert Ryle, the Oxford philosopher who died in 1976, took analysis even more narrowly to remove fundamental conceptual confusions which come from taking grammatical similarities as logical similarities. The later Wittgenstein, a profoundly influential Austrian-born critic of his own earlier work on metaphysics and logic, saw more deeply than anyone had into the connection between misleading initial propositions and the false pictures which distort them, which he called 'primitive pictures', as well as pinpointing how traditional philosophical solutions accept these pictures and the problems which they produce.

Notes

1 By G.E. Moore, in *Principia Ethica*, Cambridge, Cambridge University Press, 1903, p. vii.
2 Rudolf Carnap, 'Empiricism, Semantics and Ontology', *Revue Internationale de Philosophie* 4 (1950), pp. 20–40.
3 *Mind* n.s. XIV (1905), pp. 484–485.

Reading

*John Hospers, *An Introduction to Philosophical Analysis*, Englewood Cliffs, N.J., Prentice Hall, 1988.
Arthur Pap, *Elements of Analytic Philosophy*, New York, Macmillan, 1949.
*Richard Rorty, ed., *The Linguistic Turn: Recent Essays in Philosophical Method*, Chicago, University of Chicago Press, 1967.
Bertrand Russell, 'On Denoting', *Mind* n.s XIV (1905), pp. 479–493.
Gilbert Ryle, 'Systematically Misleading Expressions',*Proceedings of the Aristotelian Society* n.s. XXXII (1931–1932), pp. 139–170.
J.O. Urmson, *Philosophical Analysis: Its Development Between the Two World Wars*, Oxford, Oxford University Press, 1956.

The asterisk (*) in this and the suggestions for *Reading* in the following chapters indicates a comprehensive anthology or a completely authoritative introductory text.

2
Some Basic Concepts of Logic and Philosophy
What Is a Valid Argument?

A
The Concept of an Argument

In the definition of philosophy given above, philosophy was described as the attempt, by means of rational argument, to resolve a certain sort of problem. I also described what sort of problem, giving two examples. It will naturally be asked next what is meant by a rational argument. Take the following argument as an example.

Suppose	(1)	If (1) is a philosophical claim then it is just a personal opinion.
But	(2)	(1) is a philosophical claim.
So	(3)	(1) is just a personal opinion [by (1) and (2)].
But	(4)	If a good reason is available for a claim, then that claim is not just a personal opinion. (It is *more* than just a personal opinion.) [This is a definition of one sense of 'personal opinion'.]
So	(5)	If a claim is just a personal opinion, then there is no good reason available for it [by (4)].
And so	(6)	There is no good reason available for (1) [by (5) and (1)].

What does it mean to say that (1)–(6) is a rational *argument*? A minimal answer is that it is a group of propositions, one of which, called the 'conclusion' (6), follows from, or at least is meant to follow from, some of the others, which are called 'premises' [(1), (2) and (4)].

What about (3) and (5)? Are they premises or conclusions? They are derived from premises, as the justifications of each step to the right of the argument show. Thus (3) is entirely derived from (1) and (2), and (5) is entirely derived from (4). So we can say that a premise is an underived step in an argument.

(6) is the conclusion, because with it the argument ends, and it is what the argument is aimed at or what it argues for.

Here is another example of an argument, this time a more straight-forward one drawn from optics.

        (1)   If the image c is formed inside the instrument at the point where diverging rays would cross if they extended backward into the instrument, then image c is a virtual image.

        (2)   The image c is formed inside the instrument at the point where the diverging rays would cross if they extended backward into the instrument.

Therefore   (3)   The image c is a virtual image.

(1), (2) and (3) of these two arguments have the same shape or form. What this means can be shown as follows. Represent each different proposition of the first argument by a capital letter, as follows. Let 'P' represent the proposition '(1) is a Philosophical claim', and let 'O' represent '(1) is just a personal Opinion.' Then the first argument can be represented as:

        (1)   If P then O

        (2)   P

Therefore   (3)   O

In the second argument, let 'I' represent the proposition 'The Image c is formed inside the instrument at the point where the diverging rays would cross if they extended backward into the instrument' and 'V' the proposition that 'The image c is a Virtual image.' This argument can then be represented as:

        (1)   If I then V

        (2)   I

Therefore   (3)   V

Now it can be seen that the two arguments have a common form or structure. The structure is:

        (1)   If something then something else.

        (2)   Something.

Therefore   (3)   Something else.

The substitution of 'something's and 'something else's for propositions or letters representing propositions produces a representation of this form which is known as the argument-form of the arguments. We say that the two arguments have the same argument-form. Using variable lower-case letters to represent 'something's and 'something else's, the common argument-form is:

(1) If p then q
(2) p
Therefore (3) q

This argument-form is known by its Latin tag, *modus ponens*.

We have said what an argument is, and what an argument-form is. So what is a rational argument? The word 'rational' in the phrase 'rational argument' in the definition of philosophy given in Chapter 1 is an intensifier, meant to emphasize the difference between an argument in the above sense, in which the premises are or are given as the *reason* for the conclusion, and an argument in the sense in which arguments involve dispute, raised voices, bad tempers and so on, and are really quarrels. There is all the difference in the world between a discussion in which reasons are given for the claims made, and a 'discussion' which consists of anger and verbal abuse. 'Rational' marks this important difference, though the picture of a slanging match is a psychologically powerful one and easily obscures the distinction.

An argument in philosophy may raise as many questions as it answers, and this too is a function of philosophical argument. The first argument above can cause us to question the premises. Is it really the case that (1) in this argument is a philosophical claim? If not, why not? Could it be construed as a social or psychological claim? If so, is it true? On what evidence? If not, what sort of claim is it? And so on. The logic of a rational argument, on display in its argument-form, allows such questions to surface with particular clarity and force.

B
The Concept of Validity

We are now in a position to answer the question of what the validity of an argument is. We all make some sort of intuitive distinction, however rough, between what we call 'good arguments' and 'bad arguments'. We refuse to accept what we regard as bad arguments, and we believe that good arguments have an intellectual merit which bad arguments lack. We call this merit 'validity'. The problem is what validity is. What is the analysis of the following proposition?

The argument is valid.

This proposition seems to mean that in some respect what the argument says is acceptable. But:

> The Puzzle of Unacceptable Validity
> If the given argument is logically acceptable, then so is an argument having the same logical form. In that case, the following argument is also acceptable. 'If London is an animal, then London is a planet. London is an animal. So London is a planet', for it has the form *modus ponens*. But this argument is unacceptable.

The analysis of propositions about validity usually given in logic texts, which has the great merit of resolving the puzzle of unacceptable validity, goes like this. An argument is valid if the conclusion *follows from* the premises. In *modus ponens* (3) 'q' follows from (1) 'If p then q' and (2) 'p', because (1) tells us that if the truth of p is given, then so is the truth of q; and (2) tells us that the truth of p *is* given. Indeed, this can be taken to give the meaning of 'If . . . then . . .'.

This analysis of validity as the existence of the relation of *following from* between the conclusion and the premises raises the question how this further relation is to be understood. It is true that in *modus ponens* the conclusion follows the premises, in the sense that it comes lower down on the page. But the order of the premises and the conclusions in *modus ponens* can be reversed without affecting the form of argument, provided that 'therefore' is replaced with 'because' or some other equivalent such as 'since'.

	(3)	q
Because	(1)	If p then q
And	(2)	p

is also *modus ponens*.

Furthermore, there are bad arguments in which the conclusion *follows* the premises, but does not follow *from* them. It follows that these two are distinct concepts. And this is fairly obvious. A conclusion does not follow from given premises merely because it can be written down after them on the page. Any conclusion can be written down on the page after some group of premises, but not all the resulting arguments are valid.

The simplest way to understand *follows from* is that it is a relation between the conclusion and the premises of an argument, in whose argument-form the truth of the premises requires the conclusion to be true. Thus if 'If p then q' is true, and 'p' is true, then 'q' *must* be true as well.

And this is the concept of validity. An argument is valid if its conclusion follows from its premises. Its conclusion follows from its premises if it has a valid argument-form. An argument-form is valid if, given that its premises are true, its conclusion must be true as well. This has been called the 'classical conception' of validity.[1]

> The argument is a valid argument.
> ↓
> The argument has a valid argument-form.

Let this last proposition be our new initial proposition.

> The argument has a valid argument-form.
> ↓
> The argument has an argument-form which does not permit the consistent substitution of truths in its premises and a falsehood in its conclusion.

The classical conception makes a sharp distinction between the validity of an argument and the truth of its component propositions. An argument can be entirely valid, and yet consist of false propositions. 'If London is an animal, then London is a planet; London is an animal; therefore London is a planet' is an example of an argument all of whose constituent propositions are false. How then can it be a valid argument? The classical analysis of validity must be fully respected to answer this. A valid argument has a valid argument-form, in this case *modus ponens*. A valid argument-form is one in which, if the premises are true, so must the conclusion be. But this is a big 'if'. A valid argument does not ensure the truth of its conclusion, but only its truth *if* the premises are true. It *is* true of the argument 'If London is an animal, then London is a planet; London is an animal; therefore London is a planet' that *if* its premises are true, then its conclusion must be as well. But of course its premises are not true.

Here we have the resolution of the puzzle of unacceptable logical validity. The puzzle presents us with the idea that the validity of an argument is its *acceptability* or *unacceptability*, and, further, it suggests the idea that unacceptable arguments are those with which *we don't agree*. The classical analysis of validity allows us to distinguish one respect in which an argument may be acceptable, namely validity, from another respect in which it may not, namely the truth of its component propositions.

The puzzle of unacceptable validity presents a strong *picture*, the picture of someone being confronted with an apparently absurd argument, and, rightly, refusing to accept it.

Behind this picture stands another, a picture of the way in which validity attaches to an argument, just as truth does to a proposition. Suppose the truth of a proposition is its relation to a fact. Over here is the truth, there the fact.

Compare this with validity. Here is validity, there – what? To what *fact* does the validity of an argument correspond? The two pictures allow no answer, and that is one reason it can be hard to grasp the distinction between truth and validity.

C
Valid Argument-Forms and Proof

Modus ponens is a form of argument whose instances, which are arguments like the first two given at the beginning of section A of this chapter, are all valid. It is obviously not the only valid form of argument or argument-form. Here are three more.

2 *Modus Tollens*

	(1)	If p then q
	(2)	Not q
Therefore	(3)	Not p

An instance of this is:

	(1)	If Nigel Short wins the Final of the World Chess Championship against Gary Kasparov, then I'll eat my hat.
But	(2)	I won't eat my hat.
Therefore	(3)	Nigel Short won't win the Final of the World Chess Championship against Gary Kasparov.

Another instance is:

	(1)	If I go to the Weatherstone-Filliams' house for the afternoon, then I will be bored to extinction.

But   (2)   I will not be bored to extinction.
So   (3)   I'm not going.

Modus tollens is used, more or less explicitly, in much scientific argument. If relativity is true, it was argued before 1919, then light rays from a star will bend around the sun. *Modus tollens* suggested the thought that consequently if light waves from a star are found not to bend around the sun, then relativity is not true, and an expedition was organized to settle the question during a solar eclipse in South America in 1919.

Medical diagnosis offers another example. When the presence of one thing C is asserted to produce another thing S, it can be argued that since S is absent, C is also absent, or at least inactive. For example, liver disease causes protein changes in the blood. So one can argue by *modus tollens* from the absence of these changes to the absence of the disease.

3 Disjunctive Syllogism

A syllogism is simply an argument with two premises. A disjunctive syllogism is a syllogism in which one of the two premises is a disjunction. A disjunction is a proposition of the form 'p or q'. The disjunctive syllogism is a common form of argument in which two alternatives are offered. The first alternative is denied. That leaves the second. It has the form:

                (1)   p or q
                (2)   not p
Therefore   (3)   q

An instance of the disjunctive syllogism, which like many other instances has to do with alternative courses of action, is the following.

                (1)   We will stay in this house or we will leave this house this minute.
                (2)   We will not stay in this house.
Therefore   (3)   We will leave this house this minute.

The disjunctive syllogism is also a natural form of argument in many scientific, legal and medical contexts when just two possible alternatives have been established, and are recorded in the disjunctive premise.

                (1)   The defendant's sister committed the crime, or the defendant did.

(2) The defendant's sister did not commit the crime (as she was thirty miles away at the time when it was committed).

Therefore (3) The defendant committed the crime.

4 Hypothetical Syllogism

A hypothetical syllogism is one whose premises are hypothetical or conditional, containing propositions of the form 'if p then q'. What the hypothetical syllogism does is to arrange two of these conditional propositions into a chain to derive a third.

From (1) If there could be a complete theory of human behaviour, then a mischievous person could learn of such a theory.

and (2) If a mischievous person could learn of such a theory, then such a person could act in such a way as to negate it.

we get (3) If there could be a complete theory of human behaviour, then a mischievous person could act in such a way as to negate it.

One might conclude from this that there could not be such a complete theory of human nature.[2] What the hypothetical syllogism does is to cut out the middle link in a chain of three propositions. It has the self-evident form:

(1) If p then q
(2) If q then r
Therefore (3) If p then r

There are a number of other valid argument-forms, which can be put together into a system of proof. In such a system of proof, propositions given as premises yield any other proposition which is a valid conclusion from them.

It is a nice question where, so to speak, the elementary valid argument-forms like *modus ponens*, *modus tollens* and the rest 'come from'. What makes them valid? Could different argument-forms be true, say, for other cultures? The Latin tags and rather forbidding names can enhance the mystery. Consider the following four types of answer.

1 The Platonic answer (which is of the type given for this and similar problems by Plato) says that there is another world which lies beyond the material world, an unchanging world of pure forms. It is from this world that the forms of argument descend.

2   A second theory would say that logic is empirical, and that the forms of argument are like very high-level empirical generalizations of fact.
3   A third theory would regard logic as giving necessary laws of thought, rules which *define* the possibility of thought, or what thought has to be to be thought.
4   One could also see the laws of logic as taking their validity from the actual arguments which they represent, and these arguments in turn, by a process of mutual give and take (sometimes called 'reflective equilibrium'), as yielding the argument-forms.

It is interesting, however, that it does not much matter to the practice of elementary logic which of these philosophical theories we adopt.

Now to put the argument-forms to use. Suppose we are given the premises and the conclusion:

(1)   If A then B
(2)   Not B
(3)   A or C/   Therefore C

Using the above argument-forms, we can construct a simple valid proof of the conclusion in two steps as follows.

(4)   Not A [by (1) and (2) using *modus tollens*].
(5)   C [by (3) and (4) using *disjunctive syllogism*].

C has been shown to follow from 'If A then B, not B, and A or C.'

Or suppose we are given the premises:

(1)   A or, if B then C
(2)   Not A
(3)   B/   Therefore C

Using the four argument-forms given above (*modus ponens, modus tollens*, the *disjunctive syllogism* and the *hypothetical syllogism*), the reader is invited to prove or derive C from the three premises.

By means of such proofs, we can know that conclusions are true, if we know that the premises are.

Is there such a thing as a *disproof*, a way of showing that an argument is *not* valid? It will not do to try to construct a proof, and to rely on failure as a sign of invalidity. There will always be the chance that one has failed to construct the proof through lack of skill, not because it does not exist. Yet there are techniques for proving an argument invalid, if it is.

D
Proof of Invalidity by Counterexample

There are arguments which may seem to possess a valid argument-form, but in fact do not. Impressed by the power of *modus tollens*, one might argue:

> (1) If I have all my basic human rights I am free.
> (2) I do not have all my basic human rights.
> Therefore (3) I am not free.

This is a plausible-looking argument, but in fact it is not valid. (It is also not *modus tollens*, as a careful comparison with *modus tollens* will show.) Why not, and how can it be shown not to be valid?

The technique of proving invalidity has four steps.

1   Write the argument out, marking each different proposition in a different way, e.g. by underlining or double-underlining, and excluding the purely logical words 'if–then', 'not' and 'therefore' from the marking.

> (1) If <u>I do have all my basic human rights</u> then <u>I am free</u>.
> (2) <u>I do</u> not <u>have all my basic human rights</u>.
> Therefore (3) <u>I am</u> not <u>free</u>.

2   Replace the different propositions with capital letters.

> (1) If <u>R</u> then <u>F</u>.
> (2) Not <u>R</u>.
> Therefore (3) Not <u>F</u>.

3   Replace the letters for each different component proposition with lower-case variables, starting with p and going on to q, r, etc., as needed, to construct the logical form of the argument.

> (1) If p then q.
> (2) Not p.
> Therefore (3) Not q.

4   This is the critical step. Replace the ps and qs and rs with new statements, in such a way that the premises of the argument are true, and

the conclusion is false. If this can be done, the argument has been shown to be invalid, because a *counterexample* to the argument has been given. For p, substitute 'I live in Massachusetts.' For q, substitute 'I live in America.' (If the reader lives in Massachusetts, for q substitute 'I live in Alaska' instead. Readers resident in two states can work things out for themselves.)

(1) If I live in Massachusetts, then I live in America.
(2) I do not live in Massachusetts.
Therefore (3) I do not live in America.

The conclusion of the argument under 4 is false, but the premises are true. So the argument in 4 has an invalid argument-form. But we have constructed 4 so that *it has the same argument-form as the original argument* in 1.

By the classical analysis of validity given above we can say that an argument is not valid if its argument-form *does* allow a substitution instance which has true premises and a false conclusion. Accordingly the argument in 1 is not valid.

The technique of proof of invalidity by counterexample which I have given has so far been used on whole propositions. It is also possible to delve into the interior logic of the proposition, and to construct a proof of invalidity by counterexample for arguments like 'All A are B. All C are B. Therefore all A are B.' A counterexample would be 'All men (A) are human (B). All women (C) are human (B). Therefore all men (A) are women (C).'

E
Three Important Fallacies

When an argument is invalid, and therefore has a counterexample, it is sometimes called a fallacy. A *fallacy* is an error in argument. There are, however, errors of unclassifiably many different sorts, and the term 'fallacy' tends to be reserved for those errors which are psychologically convincing, or those erroneous forms of argument which mimic the patterns of valid argument, and therefore look very like them. In addition, a fallacy ought perhaps to be a common and natural error in argument, one which tends to crop up over and over again.

Fallacies are usually divided into two kinds, the informal and the formal. In the formal fallacies the form of the argument is defective or fallacious. The example of an invalid pattern of argument given above under 1–4 is thus a *formal fallacy*, and it goes under the name of *denying the antecedent*. In the conditional proposition 'If p then q', 'p' is called the *antecedent*, because it comes before (or *ante*) the logical connective 'then', and 'q' is called the *consequent*, which follows on after the 'then'.

Denying the antecedent is a psychologically plausible form which mimics *modus tollens*, but denies the wrong proposition. There is also a fallacy related to *modus ponens* which incorrectly affirms not the antecedent, as *modus tollens* does, but the consequent. This fallacy is known, naturally enough, as the fallacy of *affirming the consequent*. It has the form:

> (1) If p then q
> (2) q
Therefore (3) p

The reader is invited to construct a proof of invalidity by steps 3–4, above, for this form of argument.

There are many arguments which are formally valid, in the sense that they have a valid pattern of argument, but which yet commit an informal fallacy.

Consider, for example, the following not wholly serious argument.

> (1) Fuzzy-Wuzzy is (a) bear.
> (2) If something is bare it is not hairy.
> (3) Fuzzy-Wuzzy is not hairy.[3]

Or consider the argument that:

> (1) A box is a kind of hedge.
> (2) A match-box is a box.
Therefore (3) A match-box is a kind of hedge.

These arguments involve, among other things, the fallacy known as *equivocation*. The mistake is made when an argument depends on using a word in two different senses. The argument about Fuzzy-Wuzzy commits the fallacy in a very obvious way when it is written on the page, as the different spellings of 'bear' and 'bare' make obvious, though not when it is spoken. In the second example the two senses of 'box' are indistinguishable when written. The argument could be disambiguated by putting 'box$_1$' for 'box hedge' and 'box$_2$' for 'box container'. Then the argument would read:

> (1) A box$_1$ is a kind of hedge.
> (2) A match-box is a box$_2$.
> (3) A match-box is a kind of hedge.

So stated, the argument is formally invalid, as it has too many terms, four in all. In its original form, however, it can be classified as an informal rather than a formal fallacy.

Detecting fallacies of equivocation plays a very important role in philosophical arguments. Consider the following argument.

(1) The meaning of the word 'God' exists (it can be found in a dictionary).
(2) The meaning of the word 'God' is God (just as the meaning of the word 'dogs' is dogs – what else could it be?).
(3) God exists.

This argument is formally valid. It says that x is identical with y, that x exists, and concludes that y exists. It can be shown to be invalid, however, by substituting a counterexample with a false conclusion. If the word 'unicorn' is substituted throughout for the word 'God', for example, the argument will conclude that unicorns exist, which is, presumably, false.

So what is wrong with the argument? The answer is that it too commits the fallacy of equivocation, and commits it on the word 'meaning'. In the first premise, 'meaning' means 'dictionary-entry', or perhaps what the philosopher Frege called 'sense'.[4] In the second premise it means reference, the *object* referred to or signified by the word, or the referent of the word. Disambiguated, the argument will read as follows.

(1) The sense of the word 'God' exists.
(2) The referent of the word 'God' is God.
(3) God exists.

So formulated, the argument is clearly invalid. This does not, of course, mean that its conclusion is false, any more than it means that the conclusion is true.

Historical Note

The conscious use of refutations, arguments and proofs developed early in Greece in the fifth and fourth centuries BC. The use of variable letters to express skeletal patterns of argument is due to Aristotle, the Ancient Greek philosopher known as the 'nous' or 'mind of antiquity'. Aristotle devised the first logical system, set out in the *Prior Analytics*, dealing with arguments of two premises called *syllogisms*. Forms of argument such as *modus ponens* were given by the Stoic logicians, members of the later Greek school of Stoic philosophy, from which the English words 'stoical' and 'stoic' are derived.

Notes

1 Stephen Read, *Thinking About Logic*, Oxford, Oxford University Press, 1994, Ch. 2.
2 Or one might conclude, with Kurt Gödel, that no mischievous person will ever learn of the theory. '"Hence I conclude that such a theory exists, but that no mischievous person will learn of it. In the same way, time travel is possible, but no person will ever manage to kill his past self." Gödel laughed his laugh then ["a burst of complexly rhythmic laughter"], and concluded, "The *a priori* is greatly neglected. Logic is very powerful."' Rudy Rucker, 'Conversations with Gödel', in *Infinity and the Mind: the Science and Philosophy of the Infinite*, New York, Paladin, 1982, Ch. 4.
3 'Fuzzy-Wuzzy was a bear, / Fuzzy-Wuzzy had no hair. / Fuzzy-Wuzzy wasn't fuzzy – wuzz he?' I owe this example of equivocation to Brittin Arrington.
4 Gottlob Frege, 'On Sense and Reference', in *Philosophical Writings*, ed. and trans. Peter Geach and Max Black, Oxford, Blackwell, 1960, p. 57.

Reading

William Brenner, *Logic and Philosophy: An Integrated Introduction*, Notre Dame, Ind., University of Notre Dame Press, 1993.
*Irving Copi and Carl Cohen, *Introduction to Logic*, New York, Macmillan, 1994.
William and Martha Kneale, *The Development of Logic*, Oxford, Oxford University Press, 1978.
Stephen Read, *Thinking About Logic*, Oxford, Oxford University Press, 1994.

3
The Problem of Evil
Why Does God Allow Evil to Exist?

A
Statement of the Problem

There are a number of intuitively satisfactory but logically incomplete ways of expressing that problem in philosophy which has come to be known as 'the problem of evil'. The most common form is the question, 'Why does God allow evil?' This is not yet the problem of evil, however. For it is not a problem at all, but only a question. After all, why shouldn't God allow evil? The answer to this in the Jewish and Christian traditions is that God is supposed to be wholly good. A real problem rapidly starts to emerge.

Here is a formulation by the thirteenth-century philosopher St Thomas Aquinas.

> The Problem of Evil
> It seems that God does not exist. For if one of two contraries were infinite, the other would be altogether destroyed. But the word 'God' means that He is infinite goodness. If, therefore, God existed, there would be no evil discoverable. But there is evil in the world. Therefore God does not exist.[1]

In St Thomas' formulation a problem is stated, but it is not quite the common modern problem. For St Thomas God is a presence of infinite goodness ('He *is* infinite goodness'), not merely a being which *has* goodness. If this means that all things, without exception, and in this sense universally, or infinitely, are good, then it does contradict 'There is something which is not good' or 'There is something which is evil.' Yet St Thomas may rather mean that God's goodness is infinite. This, however, does not in any obvious way contradict the presence of evil in something other than God. Thus a surface may be perfectly flat, without preventing another surface from being rough. So God may be infinitely good; but why should this prevent *other* beings from being more or less evil?

St Thomas is working with a *picture*, the picture of goodness as a sort of stuff, like light, of which there is an infinite amount, which fills the universe. This then leaves no room for the 'contrary' stuff, which is darkness. The picture also implies some very definite relationship between God and the world. If God is light, and therefore no other thing is dark, this must be because these other things are in some way God, or dependent on God. Otherwise, the incompatibility between their darkness and his light would not be a problem. And this is confirmed by the wording of St Thomas' formulation of the problem. For he says in the passage quoted above, 'If therefore, God existed, there would be no evil discoverable. But there is evil *in the world*' (my emphasis).

The usual modern formulation of the problem, as a *dilemma*,[2] is quite a bit sharper. Here the cosmic dimension is absent, and instead God appears as a person or agent in the world, who can or cannot do things, and whose acts are to be judged as good or evil.

> Is [God] willing to prevent Evil, but not able? then is he impo-
> tent. Is he able, but not willing? then is he malevolent. Is he
> both able and willing? Whence then is Evil?[3]

The dilemma relies on the fact that in traditional Christian theology God is both good and powerful. So he is neither malevolent (which means 'ill-wishing') nor impotent (which means 'powerless' or 'lacking in power').

Another equivalent formulation is that the three propositions below form an 'inconsistent triad'. This means that any two can be true together, but not all three. With all three there is, according to the expositors of the problem, a contradiction.

> God is omnibenevolent
> God is omnipotent
> Evil exists

None of the three propositions, however, explicitly contradicts any of the others. For a contradiction is a pair of propositions with the form 'p and not-p'. But the three propositions do not have this form. They have the form 'p and q and r'.

Consider the proposition C, 'The cat sat on the mat.' Does this contradict H, 'The cat sat on the hat'? Plainly not in the sense that C and H together have the form 'p and not-p'. For C is not the negation of H.

There is, however, an implicit contradiction between C and H. It can be extracted, with the help of a quasi-logical definition, from 'the hat'. We know that, even if the hat is on the mat, or the mat is on the hat, or the mat is in the hat, then if the cat is sitting on one it is *not*, in the same sense, sitting on the other. Indeed, we could say that it is a *definition* of a hat, admittedly an absolutely minimal one, that it is not a mat, and vice versa. Or perhaps it could be regarded as an instance of a minimal definition of a material object; a material object is not any other material object. At least it is certainly true that a mat is not a hat. So then if the cat sat on only one thing, and if that one thing is the hat, then, since the mat is not the hat, the cat sat on something which was not the mat, or, in other words, the cat did not sit on the mat.

C: The cat sat on the mat. 　　H: 　　　The cat sat on the hat.
　　　　　　　　　　　　　　　　↓
　　　　　　　　　　　　　　　　A: 　　　The cat sat on something which
　　　　　　　　　　　　　　　　　　　　is not the mat (i.e. the hat).
　　　　　　　　　　　　　　　　↓
　　　　　　　　　　　　　　　　Not-C: 　The cat did not sit on the mat.

So if it is true both that the cat sat on the mat, and that the cat sat on the hat, then we have the contradiction that the cat sat on the mat and the cat did not sit on the mat, C and not-C, which has the form 'p and not-p'. So C and H are contradictory, provided the right definition of the hat is given.

In the example of the cat, the mat and the hat, the definition is 'quasi-logical' because it connects up the concept of the mat and the concept of the hat in a logical system, though it is not itself a logical concept. If what the cat sat on is the mat, then the definition tells us that what it sat on is *not* the mat. This *'not'* is a fully logical word. 'Hat' and 'cat' and 'mat', on the other hand, are words which do not belong to logic until they are brought into relationship with the logical system by a definition.

Can similar definitions be given in such a way as to make the three original propositions in the problem of evil yield up a contradiction? Are there true quasi-logical definitions of the same sort which will connect the terms of the propositions?

Suppose we define good, minimally, as the opposite of evil, as 'not evil'. So for God to want good is for him to want the opposite of evil, or to want something which is not evil. So God is in this sense opposed to evil. He wants good (he is *bene*-volent), rather than evil.

Turning to the second proposition, we can define an omnipotent being as one for whom nothing is impossible.[4] If God is omnipotent, then there is nothing he is unable to do. Or, put another way, there are no limits to God's power.[5] Thus if we were to say that God does something, as far as he is able, then, if he is omnipotent, we can delete the phrase, 'as far as he is able'. For there is in the case of an omnipotent being no 'as far as' or limit. This gives the sequence of propositions and analyses shown in Figure 1, a map of the propositional structure of the problem of evil.

The final move from 'God eliminates all evil' to 'Evil does not exist' depends on a definition of 'eliminate', to the effect that if S eliminates X, then X is eliminated by S, and X does not exist.

The problem is complete. 'Evil does not exist' contradicts 'Evil exists', and they cannot both be true. But 'Evil exists' is empirically true, if we define evil, as is often done, as physical pain, mental suffering or moral wickedness. (This does not tell us what the *concept* evil is, but merely gives examples of evils.) Hence it is false that evil does not exist. But the non-existence of evil purports to be a consequence of the two propositions about God's goodness and power.

The difficulty for theists (that is, for those who believe in the existence of a *theos*, Ancient Greek for a god) is that traditionally goodness and power are regarded as part of a list of God's defining characteristics. To give up either one would be to deny the existence of God as traditionally characterized. As J.L. Mackie observes in an important article on the problem of evil, the three main propositions 'are essential parts of most theological positions; the theologian, it seems, at once *must* adhere and *cannot consistently* adhere to all three'.[6]

Simply put, in the problem of evil it is argued that the existence of God is incompatible with the existence of evil, as in St Thomas' original formulation.

The three original propositions stand in need of analysis, and with the analysis given above, including the quasi-logical definitions, they are indeed contradictory. If so, the problem of evil cannot be resolved.

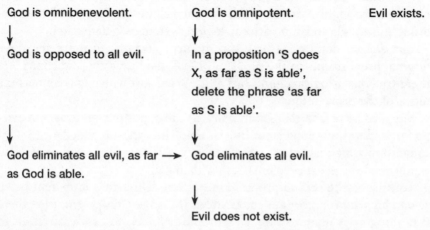

Figure 1   The Propositional Structure of the Problem of Evil

The problem of evil is itself the puzzle here, and it arises from the three original initial propositions. It is their analysis which yields the puzzle. For the theist the initial propositions can embody a strong *picture* of God's nature, which is what spurs the analysis. God is someone who does things, but only good things, and he can do anything. Also, he is goodness. Immediately, further puzzles present themselves. Why, when he does good things, is he not doing things to himself? And so on. The picture here is primitive as well as strong. If theodicy (meaning an attempt to justify God to humankind, in particular in the matter of evil) is possible, it must in part be concerned with refining these pictures. If the philosophical part of the problem can be resolved without them, it should be.

B
Three Logically Adequate
Solutions

What would it take to resolve the problem of evil? It is worth noting that the simplest solution is to deny the existence of God altogether. The problem does not exist for the atheist, who has already denied the existence of God. The problem is the conflict between the existence of God and the existence of evil, and if God does not exist, there is no conflict between his existence and the existence of anything else. The propositions stating that God is omnibenevolent and omnipotent presuppose that God exists, and, according to the atheist, this presupposition is false. So the atheist solves the problem by denying these propositions, for she or he says that nothing is omnibenevolent and omnipotent.

J.L. Mackie divides solutions to the problem of evil into two kinds: logically adequate and logically inadequate.[7] There are three main types of logically adequate solution, each one corresponding to the denial of one of the three initial propositions.

> If you are prepared to say that God is not wholly good, or not quite omnipotent, or that evil does not exist, or that good is not opposed to the kind of evil that exists, or that there are limits to what an omnipotent being can do, then the problem of evil will not arise for you.

The atheist solution could be described as a further type of solution, in which two of the three main propositions are denied.

There will also be solutions which operate by denying the quasi-logical definitions, and this would yield three more types of solution.

Taxonomy of logically adequate solutions

Type 1: Denial of God's essence
  (a) Deny omnibenevolence.
  (b) Deny omnipotence.

Type 2: Denial of God's existence
  Deny both God's omnibenevolence and omnipotence.

Type 3: Denial of the existence of evil
  Deny the existence of evil.

Type 4: Denial of the quasi-logical definitions.
  (a) Deny the proposition that God is opposed to all evil, and thereby deny that it follows from the proposition asserting God's omnibenevolence. This is a possibility, but it depends on a proposition which places it with the logically inadequate solutions, for reasons described below.
  (b) Deny the quasi-logical definition of 'omnipotent'. This is a dead end, because the quasi-logical definition simply unpacks what is in fact meant by 'omnipotent'. A 4a-type solution would therefore collapse into a 1b solution.
  (c) Deny the proposition that God eliminates all evil, as far as he is able, and so deny that it follows from God's opposition to evil. (This is taken up below in section D.)

Apart from 4c, we are left with just three main types of logically adequate solution.

1a Denial of omnibenevolence
1b Denial of omnipotence (with 2 [atheism] as a combination of 1a and 1b)
3   Denial of the existence of evil

The extent to which these logically adequate solutions are theologically almost wholly inadequate, and ultimately pointless, is interesting. The reason is that though they solve the problem of evil, they do it by a means which denies the very conception within which the problem makes sense and has its origin. This is the traditional theist's conception of God as great and good.

1a, for example, has been attempted by the psychologist Jung. In his conception of the 'quaternity' he argued that the traditional Christian Trinity must also include the devil, an evil principle, (1) because this would make it more 'whole', and (2) because of the problem of evil, and (3) because of the prevalence of religious symbolism involving four or more principles.[8]

> I cannot refrain from calling attention to the interesting fact that whereas the central Christian symbolism is a Trinity, the formula presented by the unconscious is a quaternity. In reality the orthodox Christian formula is not quite complete, because the dogmatic aspect of the evil principle is absent from the Trinity and leads a more or less awkward existence on its own as the devil.[9]

What is fundamentally and philosophically wrong with this view is that it *accepts* the picture which produces the problem. God is the substance of light, but there is also darkness. So Jung includes the darkness in the light. This solution builds *on top of* the wrongly interpreted picture, with a meaningless result. A resulting puzzle that Jung did not fully come to grips with was whether he was talking about God himself, or only the image or picture of God. Jung seemed to want to deny the former, but the latter robs his view of theological interest.

Similar observations could be made about the historically most important attempt at a solution of Type 1b. Manicheanism was a post-Christian gnostic religion, in which salvation was found through the wisdom of the light, and in which light and darkness were equally power-ful principles. Like Jung, Mani had an idiosyncratic conception of a four-fold god.

> The realm of light was bounded on three sides – to the north, to the east, and to the west. But to the south it came up against darkness. At this point then the sphere of power of the 'Father of greatness', as Mani called him, was finite.[10]

Note here too the importance of the pictorial representation. Again the philosophical question arises of what exactly is meant by 'God', if God is not completely benevolent, or not omnipotent, or both. The images of great light and activity are of no particular help, as they remain only images and not clear conceptions or definitions.

Type-3 solutions are more common, and have in various forms become a theological orthodoxy, with the Latin name *privatio boni*, the privation of good. St Augustine is the most celebrated proponent of this view. 'For what is that which we call evil but the absence of good?' Evil, he says, like a wound or a disease, 'is not a substance but a defect', or, in the philosophical jargon, an accident, with which substance is contrasted. (An accident is something which happens to something, rather than something to which something happens.) What has being or substance is good, for all being is from God. Hence non-good, or evil, is a lack of being.[11] Evil is an attack of nullity on the substances of the world.

The difficulty with this sort of view is that if God is to be exculpated and not blamed for having created evil, since evil is nothing, and hence nothing he created, he cannot be excused from the blame of having allowed nullity its power to attack substances, especially when it seems to attack some more than others. It could be said that a pot-hole is the absence of a flat paved road, but this cannot absolve the City Commissioners for Roads from their responsibility. They cannot claim that they are not responsible for the state of the roads in their cities, on the ground (so to speak) that holes have a merely negative existence. The City Commissioners cannot say that they are the Commissioners for Roads, but not for Lack of Roads. For they are also responsible for the *lack* of roads where the holes are.

In St Augustine too there is a powerful picture at work, which he describes with extraordinary clarity.

> And I sought 'whence is evil?' And sought in an evil way; nor saw I the evil in my very search. And I set in order before the view of my spirit the whole creation, and whatever we can discern in it, such as earth, sea, air, stars, trees, living creatures; yea, and whatever in it we do not see, as the firmament of heaven, all the angels, too, and all the spiritual inhabitants thereof. But these very beings, as though they were bodies, did my fancy dispose in such and such places, and I made one huge mass of all Thy creatures, distinguished according to the kinds of bodies – some of them being real bodies, some what I myself had feigned for spirits. And this mass I made huge – not as it was, which I could not know, but as large as I thought well, yet every way finite. But thee, O Lord, I imagined on every part environing and penetrating it, though every way infinite; as if there were a sea everywhere, and on every side through immensity nothing but an infinite sea; and it contained within itself some sponge, huge, though finite, so that the sponge would in all its parts be filled from the immeasurable sea ... but yet He, who is good, hath created them good, and behold how He encircleth and filleth them. Where, then, is evil, and whence, and how crept it in thither? What is its root and what its seed?[12]

And then St Augustine poses his question. 'Or hath it no being at all?' He adds, 'Why then do we fear and shun that which has no being?'

Yet in spite of his own powers of self-analysis and his realization that he was seeking evil 'in an evil way', St Augustine still *accepted* the remarkable picture of the world as a giant sea sponge, and God as the infinite sea around it. He also accepted the crude picture of God 'penetrating' the world like water in a sponge. Evil then could not be in the sponge, as the water is 'infinite' and occupies all available space. Evil must therefore be outside the sponge, and since the sponge is the world or being, evil cannot have being.

C
Four Logically Inadequate Solutions

J.L. Mackie effectively disposes of the four main solutions which are logically flawed or fallacious. His diagnosis of their fallaciousness is that in them one or more of the constituent propositions (our three initial propositions) is given up, 'but in such a way that it appears to be retained, and can therefore be asserted without qualification in other contexts'.[13]

(1) Evil is necessary as a counterpart to good.

This denies God's goodness, however. If good *requires* evil, then good, or God, is not *opposed* to evil. Furthermore, if evil is required merely as a logical contrast to good, then only a minute amount of it is necessary, not the vast amount which seems to exist.

(2) Evil is necessary as a means to good.

This denies God's omnipotence. As the cynical proverb goes, 'You can't make an omelette (good) without cracking eggs (evil).' But as God can do anything which is logically possible, he can make an omelette without cracking eggs. (It is surely not very difficult even for us to think of a way of extracting egg yolk without cracking eggs, such as osmosis or suction through a microscopic hole – not all holes are cracks.)

(3) The world is better with evil and its consequences than without it.

Yet if it is true that God is omnipotent, then he can achieve the desired consequences *without* the evil, by a different method.

Furthermore, suppose the argument given is as follows. The world with only good in it is not as good as the world with some evil in it. For evil allows an opportunity to produce more valuable or higher-order goods.

Without war, to take an extreme example, there would be no heroism and no sacrifice, which, as moral goods, are of a higher value than the physical pain and suffering produced by war.

Schematically, at the first level, a world without evil – call it world$_1$ – has a goodness of 1. In this world:

$$G_1 = 1.$$

If we introduce evil, we get a worse result, a world$_2$ in which:

$$(G_1 + E_1) = 0,$$

which is less than 1. So God, being good, would obviously choose the better world, world$_1$.

However, world$_2$ allows a possibility which world$_1$ does not. World$_2$ allows the development of a greater good, G_2, which is brought into being by the opposing E_1. We can represent this by a rule according to which $(E_1 \rightarrow G_2)$, where G_2 is a higher-order or greater good. So the complete sum in world$_2$ is:

$$(G_1 - E_1) + G_2 = 2.$$

Accordingly world$_2$ is better than world$_1$, and God would choose it.

This argument overlooks two things. In the first place, it is hardly obvious that the moral goods which result from the existence of evil really do add up to as much as twice the good in a world without evil. Second, and more seriously, the argument does not include second-order evil. War can certainly bring heroism and moral goodness of a high order, but it can also bring cowardice, betrayal and despair, and other second-order evils. Thus the real sum for world$_2$ should be:

$$(G_1 - E_1) + (G_2 + E_2),$$

and this of course = 0. So the question why world$_2$ is better than world$_1$, in which $G_1 = 1$, has not been answered.

(4)   Evil is necessary as a precondition for freewill.

The idea here is that freewill is such a very great good that no precondition is too great a price to pay for it. The greatest possible good (G) requires human freewill (F). Freewill requires choice (C). Choice requires good (G) *and* evil (E).

$G \rightarrow F$
$F \rightarrow C$
$C \rightarrow (G \text{ and } E)$.

Hence, by two hypothetical syllogisms:

$G \rightarrow (G \text{ and } E)$,

and hence:

$G \rightarrow E$.

Mackie questions the last premise. Why should choice require evil as well as good, exactly?

> [I]f God has made men such that in their free choices they sometimes prefer what is good and sometimes what is evil, why could he not have made men such that they always freely choose the good? If there is no logical impossibility in a man's freely choosing the good on one, or on several, occasions, there cannot be a logical impossibility in his freely choosing the good on every occasion.[14]

The last argument here seems weak. If there is no logical impossibility in claiming that just one angle of a triangle is a right angle, does it follow that there cannot be a logical impossibility in claiming that every angle is a right angle? If there is no logical impossibility in a man's eating the food on just one, or on several, occasions, then by Mackie's argument there cannot be a logical impossibility in his eating the food on every occasion – throughout the day. But perhaps there is.

Yet Mackie's argument as a whole seems sound. Let there be a roulette wheel, which, purely by chance, always gives number 21. The probability that such a wheel does not exist is enormous (or infinite: $37 \times 37 \times 37 \times 37 \times 37 \times 37 \dots$, depending on whether 'always' means 'at all times' or 'whenever it is spun', and, if the latter, how many times that is). One might suspect, very reasonably, after a dozen or so spins, that the wheel was not free, or that it was rigged, as we say, but suppose this is not the case. The pattern of the numbers (N, N, N, N . . .) is certainly an unusual one, but, as it is said, the wheel has no memory (unless it is rigged), and any individual sequence of numbers is as improbable as any other. There is no contradiction in the description of a wheel which on just one occasion gives number 21, and there is no contradiction in the description of a wheel which gives number 21 on all occasions, even if the second non-contradiction does not follow from the first.

D
The Logic of the Argument

The logically adequate solutions are theologically inadequate to the point of extreme heterodoxy, and they take the pictures they invoke beyond anything their logic can support. The theologically adequate solutions are logically inadequate, as Mackie has shown. So it would seem that *theos* (God) and *logos*, including logic, are incompatible. The English word 'logic' is derived from the Greek word *logos*, which means 'reason', 'explanation', 'word' and 'speech'. *Logos* is also applied by Christians to Jesus, the second person of the trinity, especialy in the Gospel of St John. So to claim that *theos* and *logos* are incompatiable would, in this last sense, be to deny the incarnation of God in human form as Jesus. Theologically, however, *logos* and *theos* are not incompatiable, and I shall try to show that this is also true from a logical point of view.

I begin by supposing, as we have already done, that the proposition that evil exists is factually true, and that on this point Christian Science and St Augustine are alike mistaken, for the reasons given above. So:

	(1)	Evil exists.
So	(2)	It is false that evil does not exist.
	(3)	If God eliminates all evil then evil does not exist [from Figure 1].
So	(4)	God does not eliminate all evil [by (3), (2), *modus tollens*].
	(5)	If God eliminates all evil, as far as he is able, and he is omnipotent, then God eliminates all evil [from Figure 1].
So	(6)	It cannot both be true that God eliminates all evil, as far as he is able, and that he is omnipotent [by (5), (4), *modus tollens*].
But	(7)	God is omnipotent [from Figure 1].
So	(8)	God does not eliminate all evil, as far as he is able [from (6) and (7)].

Figure 1 tells us that:

(9) If God is opposed to all evil, then God eliminates all evil, as far as he is able.

However, assuming that:

(10) God is opposed to all evil (as it follows from the intitial proposition that he is omnibenevolent),

it follows that

> (11)   The proposition that God eliminates all evil, as far as he
> is able, *does not follow from the proposition that he is
> opposed to all evil*!

What this means is that the proposition that God eliminates all evil, as
far as he is able, is not the analysis of the proposition that he is opposed to
all evil.

This negative point locates the source of the problem of evil in false
analyses of the relevant initial propositions, as well as in the false pictures
associated with them. With two theologically reasonable assumptions, that
is, assumptions as reasonable as theology itself, the propositions that God
is good and great, we have reached the conclusion that if God exists both
(1) God is opposed to evil, and (2) he does not eliminate evil.

Attempted elimination is one form of opposition, but not the only one.
The distinction between opposition and elimination is logically more
powerful than the contradiction derived from the initial propositions, for
without the distinction there is no contradiction. So there is a clear sense
in which the puzzle, the problem of evil, arises from interpretations of the
initial propositions which require the proposition that God eliminates evil,
such as the picture of God as light, the eliminator of darkness, in St Thomas, or of St Augustine's image of the giant sea *spongia*. What is left of
the problem is theological, and will hinge on what one's conception of God
is. 'What is the characteristic mode of God's activity, opposition but not
instant elimination, which explains the gap between the proposition that
God is opposed to evil and the proposition that he does not eliminate it'
would be one Christian, though not only a Christian, formulation of the
resulting theological question.

Historical
Note

The main statements of the problem are found in the Jewish and Christian
tradition of belief in a just and loving God. The Old Testament Book of Job
contains the archetypal story of a just man assailed by evil. Plotinus, in
The Enneads, and St Augustine, in the *Confessions*, are the main classical
expositions. Many other philosophers in the history of the subject have
discussed the problem, most notably St Thomas Aquinas, Leibniz and
Hume. Purely religious thinkers have tended to blame evil on the Fall
of Man. The twentieth century has seen much passionate and detailed

philosophical discussion, especially in the light of war and genocide, with no single view commanding universal assent.

Notes

1 St Thomas Aquinas, *Summa Theologica*, trans. Fathers of the English Dominican Province, Ottawa, Collège Dominicain d'Ottawa, 1941, First Part, Q2 Art. 3.
2 A dilemma argues from the premises: if p then q, and if r then s, but p or r, so q or s.
3 David Hume, *Dialogues Concerning Natural Religion*, ed. John Vladimir Price, Oxford, Oxford University Press, 1976, pp. 226–227.
4 With the exception, in some theologies, including St Thomas', of what is incoherent or contradictory. There is a sense in which this exception is not an exception at all. It is no limit to God's intelligence that he cannot solve a problem which has been badly posed or has no solution because it has been misdescribed. So it is no limit on his power that he cannot do something impossible, as there is a sense in which nothing has been coherently specified or described for him to do. What is at fault is not his power, but our description of what we are inviting him to do.
5 The sense of note 4, above, can be expressed by saying that the logically impossible is not a limit on the possible.
6 J.L. Mackie, 'Evil and Omnipotence', *Mind* lxix, No. 254 (1955), p. 200.
7 Ibid., pp. 201–202.
8 For a denial that Jung is right about this, see H.L. Philp, *Jung and the Problem of Evil*, New York, Robert McBride, 1958, p. 74ff.
9 C.G. Jung, *The Collected Works*, Vol. 11, *Psychology and Religion: West and East*, trans. R.F.C. Hull, London, Routledge, 1958, pp. 59–60.
10 Geo Widengren, *Mani and Manichaeism*, trans. Charles Kessler, London, Weidenfeld and Nicolson, 1961, p. 47.
11 St Augustine, *The Confessions*, trans. J.G. Pilkington, New York, Liveright, 1943, Book VII, Ch. 5.
12 Ibid.
13 Mackie, 'Evil and Omnipotence', p. 201.
14 Ibid, p. 209. See the reply by Ninian Smart, 'Omnipotence, Evil and Supermen', *Philosophy* xxxvi, No. 137 (1961), pp. 188–195, attacking the view that God could create free men who would not sin.

Reading

John Hick, *Philosophy of Religion*, Englewood Cliffs, N.J., Prentice Hall, 1983.
C.G. Jung, *Answer to Job: The Problem of Evil: Its Psychological and Religious Origins*, trans. R.F.C. Hull, New York, Meridian, 1960.
G.W. Leibniz, *Theodicy: Essays on the Goodness of God, the Freedom of Man and the Origin of Evil*, London, Routledge, 1951.
J.L. Mackie, 'Evil and Omnipotence', *Mind* lxix, No. 254 (1955).
*Nelson Pike, ed., *God and Evil: Readings in the Theological Problem of Evil*, Englewood Cliffs, N.J., Prentice Hall, 1964.

4
The Existence of God
Can the Existence of God Be Proved?

A
The Ontological Argument

The upshot of the previous chapter is that the existence of God is logically compatible with the existence of evil. So it is false that the existence of evil makes belief in the existence of God positively *irrational*. The existence of evil does not contradict belief in the existence of God.

It is one thing to say that belief in the existence of God is not irrational, because the proposition that evil exists does not, by itself, logically count *against* the belief. It is quite another thing to say that the belief is rational, in the sense that a positive reason can be given *for* it.

Many reasons and arguments have been given for belief in the existence of the God of the monotheistic religions. The argument to be discussed in this chapter is taken from the second chapter of a work called the *Proslogion*, written by St Anselm of Canterbury in the eleventh century. It was dubbed the 'ontological argument' in the eighteenth century, though this might be thought to be something of a misnomer, as 'ontological' means having to do with existence, and in the end all proofs of God's existence have to do with existence. Still, the argument does hinge on a comparison between a world in which God exists, and a world in which he is thought not to. What follows is not the text of St Anselm's argument, but a reconstruction of part of it which aims to make the sequence of the steps, including the crucial 'ontological' one, as clear as possible.

> (1)   God is a being, *than which no greater can be conceived or is possible.*

This is St Anselm's definition of God. God is the greatest being, and none greater can be conceived or is possible. In the terms of our earlier formulation of the problem of evil, the definition (1) centres on God being *omni*-everything he is. He is powerful, but he is also omnipotent. He knows, but he is also omniscient. He is benevolent, but also omnibenevolent. St Anselm's (1) is an analysis of the term 'God'.

> God exists
> ↓
> A being, *than which no greater can be conceived or is possible*, exists.

To continue with the ontological argument:

Suppose   (2)   A being, *than which no greater can be conceived or is possible*, does not exist.

But then   (3)   A being greater than the being, *than which no greater can be conceived or is possible*, can be conceived or is possible.

How so? Well, it turns out that a being greater than the one *than which no greater can be conceived or is possible*, which, by supposition (2), does not exist, *can* be conceived and so shown to be possible after all, namely, a being *than which no greater can be conceived or is possible* which *does* actually exist!

But (3) contains a contradiction. Hence the supposition (2), from which it follows, is false. But if (2) is false, then it must be true that:

            (4)   A being, *than which no greater can be conceived or is possible*, does exist.

So   (5)   God exists [by (4) and (1)].

The heart of this argument is what is called an indirect proof or a *reductio ad absurdum* proof, sometimes simply known as a *reductio*. A proof of this sort begins by assuming the *opposite* of what it sets out to prove. In the argument above, this happens at step (2), the 'ontological' step. The next step is to deduce an 'absurdity' or contradiction from this assumption. This is (3). The final step is to conclude the *opposite* of the original assumption. This happens at (4). With the definition given in (1), St Anselm then draws his conclusion, (5).

Here is another indirect or *reductio* argument, this time from arithmetic, not theology. It is a proof that there is no largest number. Let us call the largest number, if there is one, L.

(1)   L is a number, *than which no larger can be conceived or is possible*.

Suppose   (2)   The number, *than which no larger can be conceived or is possible*, exists.

But then   (3)   A number larger than the number, *than which no larger can be conceived or is possible*, can be conceived or is possible.

How so? Well, it turns out that a number larger than the one *than which no larger can be conceived or is possible* after all *can* be conceived and so shown to be possible, simply by conceiving a number formed by adding 1 to L, and generating a new number, L + 1!

But (3) is a contradiction. Hence the supposition (2), from which it follows, is false. But if (2) is false, then it must be true that:

(4)   The number, *than which no larger can be conceived or is possible*, does not exist.

So   (5)   L does not exist [by (4) and (1)].

These two arguments are arranged to make their parallel structures evident. There is one big dissimilarity, though. The indirect argument about L has a *negative* conclusion; it concludes that L *does not* exist. The ontological argument has a positive conclusion; it concludes that God *does* exist.

This dissimilarity raises the question of whether the ontological argument illegitimately assumes at the outset that there *is* a greatest being. Does the ontological argument *assume* that a hierarchy of beings ascending in greatness is *unlike* the hierarchy of numbers ascending in largeness just in that there is a highest member of the hierarchy of beings? And does this assume *exactly* what the argument sets out to prove, namely that *there is* or *there exists* a highest member of the hierarchy, a greatest being, than which no greater can be conceived or is possible?[1]

A line of thought deriving from the comparison between the ontological argument and indirect arguments like the one against L was noticed by Leibniz in his 'Two Notations for a Discussion with Spinoza' of 1676.[2] He pointed out that the notion of the greatest being might be like the notion of the greatest speed in the following crucial respect. The latter notion, according to him, is not consistent. Call this greatest speed S.

(1)   S is a speed, *than which no greater can be conceived or is possible*.

Suppose   (2)   The speed, *than which no greater can be conceived or is possible*, exists.

But then   (3)   A speed greater than the speed, *than which no greater can be conceived or is possible*, can be conceived or is possible.

How so? The answer is that a speed greater than the one *than which no greater can be conceived or is possible* can after all be achieved. Consider a wheel which turns with the supposedly greatest conceivable speed S.[3] Let there be a wheel which is turning at this speed. Now imagine adding an extension onto one of the spokes of the wheel straight out beyond the rim. The rim is turning at S. But the point at the end of the new extension has to cover a greater distance than a corresponding point on the rim, in the same time. Hence the point at the end of the extension is travelling at a faster speed than the rim, which is travelling at S. For speed is distance travelled in a given time. The speed of the point at the end of the extension is greater than S, and so there is a speed greater than S, the supposed speed *than which no greater can be conceived or is possible*.[4]

        (4)   The speed, *than which no greater can be conceived or is possible*, does not exist.

So   (5)   S does not exist [by (4) and (1)].

So Leibniz set himself the task of showing that the notion of a single greatest possible being is consistent, unlike the notions of a largest number L or a greatest possible speed S. He tried to do this by showing that it cannot be the case that a greatest being cannot exist, and he gave a general argument for this conclusion.

The argument begins with the definition of a perfection as a sort of *positive maximum or absolute*, or, as Leibniz put it, one which 'expresses' whatever it does express 'without limits', or absolutely. Being positive excludes the possession of anything evil in St Augustine's privative or negative sense. Omnipotence is a perfection, because something omnipotent expresses power without limit. There is no limit to what an omnipotent being can do. Complete and absolute impotence, or *omni-impotence* as it might be called, would not count as a perfection, because it is negative (*im*potence), even though it is absolute and maximal.

Leibniz also says in this proof that a perfection is simple or irresolvable. By this he means that the term for a perfection cannot be defined or further resolved into simpler terms, as for example 'murder' can be resolved into the further terms 'unlawful act', 'intentional act' and 'killing'.

Suppose, Leibniz argues, that two perfections, A and B (defined as simple, absolute and positive), are incompatible. A and B are by the definition irresolvable. But if they are incompatible, they can be resolved.

Therefore A and B are compatible.

If the cat cannot sit on the mat and the hat at the same time, that is, if the mat and the hat cannot coexist in the same subject (the sitting cat), then there must be a logical relation between them, to be given in the form of a partial resolution of the proposition which in Chapter 3 we called H, 'The cat sat on the hat', into 'The cat sat on something which is not the mat'. (It is 'partial' because there is, positively, quite a bit more to being a hat than not being a mat.)

Leibniz's contribution to the ontological argument was that he offered a proof to show that the notion of a greatest being is consistent, unlike the notions of the greatest number and the greatest speed.

B
Gaunilo: Invalidity by Counterexample

The earliest criticism of St Anselm's argument was made by a fellow monk, Gaunilo.[5] Gaunilo's argument took the form of an attempt to prove St Anselm's argument invalid by constructing a counterexample.

	(1)	P is an island, *than which no greater can be conceived or is possible*.
Suppose	(2)	An island, *than which no greater can be conceived or is possible*, does not exist.
But then	(3)	An island greater than an island, *than which no greater can be conceived or is possible*, can be conceived or is possible.

How so? Well, it turns out that an island greater than the one *than which no greater can be conceived or is possible*, which by supposition (2) does not exist, *can* be conceived or is possible after all, namely one which *does* exist!

But (3) is a contradiction. Hence the supposition (2), from which it follows, is false. But if (2) is false, then it must be true that:

	(4)	An island, *than which no greater can be conceived or is possible*, does exist.
So	(5)	P exists [by (4) and (1)].

The point of this counterexample is of course that we know perfectly well that P does not exist. The structure of the argument will allow for an argument proving the existence of absolutely anything, provided we tack onto it the word 'perfect'. (Question: is it true of what any term refers to that it *makes sense* to call it perfect? Does the idea of a perfect teapot, for example, make sense? Or a perfect neutron?)

So the conclusion (5) is false, and, assuming that the premises are true, it follows that the argument is invalid. But if the argument is invalid, then so is the ontological argument, because it has the same argument-form. Or so goes the criticism of St Anselm's argument by Gaunilo.

Yet there is a difficulty with the counterexample. Consider (1) in the ontological argument, and compare it to the other parallel (1)s in the arguments against L and S and in Gaunilo's counterexample. (1) contains an ellipsis, an omission. What it means is that God is a being, than which no greater *being* can be conceived or is possible. Filling in the ellipses in the other parallel propositions, we get:

> God is a being, than which no greater *being* can be conceived or is possible.
> L is a number, than which no larger *number* can be conceived or is possible.
> S is a speed, than which no greater *speed* can be conceived or is possible.

How should (1) in Gaunilo's counterexample be analysed? There are two possibilities.[6]

(a) P is an island, than which no greater *island* can be conceived or is possible.
(b) P is an island, than which no greater *being* can be conceived or is possible.

Which of these two is the correct analysis of Gaunilo's Counterexample? Take (a) first. Russell Wahl has also pointed out that the (a)-interpretation is decisively supported by Gaunilo's own text. Gaunilo refers to 'this island which is more excellent than all *lands*' (Wahl's emphasis).[7]

So we have:

> (1a) P is an island *than which no greater [island] can be conceived or is possible.*

The trouble with 1(a) is that it will not fall within the scope of Leibniz's proof. The greatest island will be susceptible to improvement or change for the better, and also for the worse – a new airport, perhaps – just as the greatest number and the most rapid motion are susceptible to change for the larger. Leibniz's argument doesn't work with the (a)-substitution, which means that the greatest island is not possible.

Furthermore, the greatest island does not have all perfections, but only those appropriate and proper to *islands*. 'Being' is the key term in the original argument, and the (a)-substitution removes it. So what about (1) in Gaunilo's counterexample with (b)?

> (1b)   P is an island *than which no greater [being] can be conceived or is possible.*

Here there are two problems.

1   First, (1b) does not have the same logical form as (3) in the original ontological argument. Compare:

> (1)   God is a being, *than which no greater being can be conceived or is possible.*
> (1b)   P is an island, *than which no greater being can be conceived or is possible.*

The pattern of terms in (1) ('being', 'greater being') does not match the pattern in (1b) ('island', 'greater being', and so Gaunilo's counterexample is not a counterexample at all, and his proof of invalidity fails.

2   The second problem is that though (1a) is true if there is an island *than which no greater [island] can be conceived,* under this same condition (1b) is false. Even if there is an island *than which no greater can be conceived or is possible,* there must yet be in the universe greater things than this greatest island, for example the greatest archipelago, which has many islands, all of them presumably perfect.

Let us turn to a disanalogy between the logical forms *being a (perfect) being* and *being a (perfect) island,* a disanalogy which cuts the other way, against the ontological argument rather than against the argument against the ontological argument. I shall call the objection to the ontological argument 'the standard objection'. It has been championed in different versions by philosophers as different as St Thomas Aquinas, Hume, Kant and Bertrand Russell.

C
The Standard Objection

In this section I will consider an objection to the ontological argument. This objection is made against a form of the argument which was given in the seventeenth century by Descartes. Descartes is known as the father of modern philosophy, but in this argument he looks back to medieval philosophy and theology.

	(1)	God has all perfections [= has all 'greatnesses'].
	(2)	Existence is a perfection [= if something exists it is greater than if it does not].
So	(3)	God has existence [= God exists].[8]

In *The Critique of Pure Reason*, Kant advanced the objection that '"*Being*" [or existence] is obviously not a real predicate.'[9] He meant that 'being' or 'exists' does not belong on a list of predicates, that is, things said *about* the subject. Of God, for example, we can predicate goodness, wisdom and power.

God is good
wise
powerful

Now, says Kant, 'the small word "is" adds no new predicate, but only serves to posit the predicate *in its relation* to the subject'. It is obvious that we cannot add 'the small word "is"' as a predicate on the same list as 'good', 'wise' and 'powerful', because then we would get the nonsensical proposition that 'God is is.' Perhaps this could be construed theologically (cf. 'I am that I am'), but in the absence of some such context it makes no sense. Yet when Kant tells us that 'the small word' cannot be added to the list of predicates, he also means that we cannot add equivalents like 'exists' (which would have to appear in the substantive form of 'existent') to the list of predicates. He says that:

> If, now, we take the subject (God) with all its predicates (among which is omnipotence), and say 'God is' or 'There is a God', we attach no new predicate to the concept of God, but only posit the subject in itself with all its predicates, and indeed posit it as being an *object* that stands in relation to my *concept*.

To say that an object *a* exists is not to say that *a* has the predicate or property or characteristic of existing. For what is it that has this predicate?

If it is *a*, then it must exist in order to be capable of receiving the predicate. To say that the cat has fatness is to say of something which is assumed to exist, the cat, that some predicate is true of it. Then it has already been assumed that the cat exists, and it is redundant to add a predicate to this effect in addition to the copula. (A copula is an equational verb like 'is' which links the subject and predicate of a sentence.)

So for Kant the following analysis is false.

a exists.
↓
The predicate 'existent' is true of *a*.

The puzzle behind this analysis, which I shall call the 'classical analysis of existence', is the problem of negative existentials, which already plagued the early Greek philosophers.

> The Puzzle of the Necessary Falsehood of Negative Existential Propositions
> Existence cannot be a predicate of what is said to exist, *a*. For then to *deny* that *a* exists would be to say that it lacks the predicate 'exists'. But since it does not exist, this cannot be the case, as there is nothing to lack the predicate! To say that unicorns do not exist would be to say, on the analysis, *of unicorns*, that *they* do not exist. But if the classical analysis of existence is true with 'unicorns' substituted for '*a*', then there are no unicorns to say this of! '*This* does not exist', said of an indicated object, must always be false, and no negative existential proposition can ever be true. If reference is secured for the subject, a denial of its existence must be false.

There is also the opposite problem.

> The Puzzle of the Necessary Truth of Positive Existential Propositions
> Existence cannot be a predicate of what is said to exist, *a*. For then to *affirm* that *a* exists would be to say that it possesses the predicate 'exists'. But since it must *already* exist to receive the predicate, this cannot be the case. Any statement that *a* exists is bound to be true, as *a* has been antecedently identified. '*This* exists' must always be true, and no affirmative existential proposition can ever be false. If reference is secured for the subject, an assertion of existence *must* be true.

The analysis of existence for which Kant is arguing is the successful 'positing of an object under a concept', or the satisfaction of the concept by an object. To say that cats exist is not to predicate the existence of cats, but to assert, of the *concept* 'cat', that it has an object. In this solution to the two puzzles the concept 'cat' provides the pre-existing platform from which one can deny the existence of cats, or affirm their existence without the risk of necessarily being right. According to this analysis, to assert or deny the existence of cats is not to state a proposition about cats, but to affirm of the *concept* 'cat' that it has one or more objects. To deny that cats exist is to affirm that the concept 'cat' has no object.

> *a* exists.
> ↓
> The concept '*a*' has an object.

According to Kant, the Cartesian ontological argument depends on the first of these two analyses, the classical analysis of existence. The second premise of the Cartesian ontological argument presupposes that existence is a property or predicate, as perfections are properties of what they are predicated of. Yet Kant's own analysis is uninformative and circular. For 'has an object' must mean 'has an object *which exists*', and the last clause is still in need of analysis.

> The concept '*a*' has an object.
> ↓
> The concept '*a*' has an object which exists.

But this says:

> *a*, which is the object of which '*a*' is the concept, exists.

Suppressing the subordinate clause 'which is the object of which "*a*" is the concept', we get

> *a* exists.

We have come round in a circle back to the original proposition to be analysed.

Let us look at a better analysis of existence, due to Bertrand Russell. In the Cartesian ontological argument, (1) says that God has all those properties or predicates which are perfections, such as goodness, wisdom and the rest. (2) says that on this list of predicates is to be found existence. This is the classical analysis. So the ontological argument depends on the classical analysis. But then we are faced with the puzzle of negative existential propositions and the puzzle of the necessity of positive existential propositions. What Russell did in his celebrated 'On Denoting' of 1905 was to give an analysis of what he called 'denoting phrases', such as 'a man', 'the man', 'the centre of mass of the solar system' and so on, which resolved several apparently unrelated puzzles, including the problem of negative existentials.

According to Russell's analysis, phrases like 'the mythical one-horned horse', 'the present King of France', 'the perfect island' and so on are 'denoting phrases which do not denote anything'. Russell included proper names within the scope of this analysis by arguing that names are disguised descriptions. 'A proposition about Apollo means what we get by substituting what the classical dictionary tells us is meant by Apollo, say "the sun-god".'[10]

How did Russell's analysis handle negative existential propositions like 'The golden mountain does not exist', which creates the puzzle of the necessary falsehood of negative existential propositions?

> The golden mountain does not exist.
> ↓
> '"x is golden" and "x is a mountain" are both false' is always true.

Or, in other words, if someone says that something is both golden and a mountain, she or he is always wrong. It is not jointly true of any x that x is golden and that x is a mountain.

Let the capital letters 'A' and 'B' stand for the properties or predicates of *a*, such as the properties or predicates 'Greek' and 'sun-god', which are true of Apollo, or 'golden' and 'mountain', which are true of the golden mountain. Then we get the following analysis.

> *a* exists.
> ↓
> '"x is A" and "x is B" are both false' is not always true.

What has happened here is that the name '*a*' has been analysed as the joint description 'the (thing which is) A and B', and this in turn analysed as the assertion of the joint truth of the predications on at least one occasion. Russell's theory solves our two puzzles about existential propositions easily. In Russell's analysis of '*a* exists' the term '*a*' occurs within quotation marks, and so it does not need to refer to anything for the whole analysis to be true. In 'He said, "Unicorns exist"', and 'He said that unicorns exist', the term 'unicorns' does not need to refer to anything for the proposition to be true.

I wish now to turn Russell's theory against Kant's argument that exist-ence is not a real predicate. Russell himself took his argument to have the opposite effect, but I am suggesting he misjudged the import of his own theory. Consider again the three predicates given of God. God is good; God is wise; God is powerful. If the three predicates remain uncombined, as in Russell's analysis, that is, if no x is all good, all wise and all powerful, then God does not exist. What follows? If God does exist, the predicates *are* combined. Let us take this as the *analysis* of '*a* exists.'

> *a* exists.
> ↓
> *a*'s predicates (A, B, C . . .) are combined.

This says that the existence of an object is the conjunction or combin-ation of the predicates. So we have a list of predicates, the combination of which *is* the existence of the object to which the predicates apply.

> *a*   is   A
>   B
>   C
>   .
>   .
>   .

Kant is right that 'existent' or 'exists' will not be found on this list, as it is already given in the copula 'is'. But he is right for the wrong reason. The predicate 'exists' will not be found *on* the list, because it *is* the list, the joint satisfaction of the predicates A, B, C . . . . When the predicates are joined together, that is, whatever their joint truth constitutes, is some-thing which exists. And the other way around, whatever exists is a joint predication.

But Kant is wrong to say that 'existent' is not a real predicate because it does not appear on the list of predicates. It is not, as he thinks, a grammat-ical condition for the application of *any* predicate, but a consequence of the logical fact of the combination or joint satisfaction of *all* the predicates. 'Existent' is the totality of all the predicates, and this is what it is for a subject *a* to exist. The classical analysis needs modification. 'Existent' is not a predicate, it is *the* predicate, meaning by this the conjunction of all *a*'s predicates. So the predicate 'existent' *is a*. The subject *a* is *the existent*! How can this be?

How can it be that the single predicate, 'existent', *is* a subject, namely *a*? The answer is that this predicate is in fact a *group* of predicates, A, B, C and so on. So the classical analysis can be extended.

The predicate 'existent' is true of *a*.
↓
The list of predicates A, B, C . . . is *a*.

The analysis now says that a subject is a group of predicates. This has the neat consequence that what it is for a predicate A to attach to a subject *a*, or 'inhere' in *a*, to use the classical jargon, is for A to be on the list of predicates which jointly constitute *a*. There could hardly be a simpler and prettier solution to a difficult puzzle ('the problem of inherence') than this.

How does the modified classical analysis solve the puzzles about existence and non-existence? First, there is the problem of the necessary falsehood of negative existential propositions. Question: what secures the reference for '*a*', the term, when *a* does not exist and we wish to say so? Answer: the totality of predicates. We are then saying that the individual predicates do *not* form a group which is jointly true. The existent – the joint list of predicates – is denied.

Second, there is the problem of the necessary truth of positive existential propositions. Question: what secures the reference for '*a*' when *a* does exist, in such a way as not to make this and every other affirmative existential statement true? Answer: the totality or joint list of predicates.

An example will help here. Consider a prime number P which lies between 10 and 12. This number exists; it is 11. What has been said when it has been said that this number exists? Let the predicates of P be 'is a whole number', '>10', '<12', and 'is prime'. What has been said when it has been said that P exists is that 'is a whole number' is jointly satisfied or true with '>10', that these two are jointly satisfied with '<12', and that this group is jointly satisfied with 'is prime'. 'The existent' – the list of predicates – is affirmed.

Is the ontological argument sound? If it is not, it is not for the Kantian reasons which we have examined. The most common intuitive reaction against the argument is that it is pure thought spinning out of itself truths about the real world but unchecked by the real world.[11] Yet this is exactly what happens in the case of pure mathematics, and also, in a different but what can in some moods seem to us an equally surprising way, in the case of art.

What then must we be assuming about reality which makes us intuitively believe that this cannot happen in the case of theology, the study of *theos*? And what are we thereby assuming about the nature of the relationship between thought and reality? This relationship is easily represented in pictures which are false.

Historical Note

The ontological argument has been much discussed since St Anselm for-mulated it in the eleventh century and St Thomas Aquinas rejected it in the thirteenth. It was adopted by the three great rationalist philo-sophers Descartes, Spinoza and Leibniz, in the sixteenth and seventeenth centuries, and dubbed 'the ontological proof' in the eighteenth century by Kant (because it hinges on the treatment of the concept of existence). In *The Critique of Pure Reason* Kant declared the argument 'so much labour and effort lost'. In the twentieth century it has seen something of a revival, gaining support from the notable American philosophers Charles Hartshorne and Norman Malcolm.

Notes

1 An interesting new puzzle is this.
   The Puzzle of the Disanalogy of Orders of Numbers and of Beings
   If the hierarchy of numbers fails to end in L, and has no final end, then the hierarchy of beings ordered by greatness has no final end, either.
   A question for the alert student unwilling to be seduced by the picture of an analogy between a hierarchy of numbers and a hierarchy of beings: is there a fallacy in the following argument: 'Numbers are all beings, so how can what is true of numbers fail to be true of all beings?'? ('Cats are all beings, and cats are rough-tongued, so all beings are rough-tongued.')

2 The passage is reprinted in Alvin Plantinga, ed., *The Ontological Argument from St Anselm to Contemporary Philosophers*, New York, Doubleday, 1965, pp. 54–56, where its origin is incorrectly given as Leibniz's *New Essays Concerning Human Under-standing* rather than Gottfried Wilhelm Leibniz, 'Two Notations for a Discussion with Spinoza', in *Philosophical Papers and Letters*, ed. L.E. Loemker, Dordrecht, Reidel, 1956, p. 293.

3 Gottfried Wilhelm Leibniz, 'Meditations on Knowledge, Truth and Ideas', in *Philo-sophical Papers and Letters*, p. 293.

4 This makes one want to know the logico-physical status of a wheel turning at the speed of light, which is according to physicists the maximum speed of anything in the uni-verse. How fast will a point at the end of a one-atom extension to this wheel be turning?

5 Plantinga, *Ontological Argument*, pp. 13ff.

6 William E. Mann, 'The Perfect Island', *Mind* lxxxv, No. 339 (1976), pp. 417–421.

7 Plantinga, *Ontological Argument*, p. 11.

8 René Descartes, 'Meditations on First Philosophy', *The Philosophical Writings of Des-cartes*, Vol. II, ed. and trans. John Cottingham, Robert Stoothof and Dugald Murdoch, Cambridge, Cambridge University Press, 1984, pp. 45–46. See also p. 117 in the 'Objec-tions and Replies': To say that something is contained in the nature or concept of a thing is the same as saying that it is true of that thing. But necessary existence is contained in the concept of God. Therefore it may be truly affirmed of God that necessary existence belongs to him, or that he exists.'

9 Plantinga, *Ontological Argument*, p. 62.
10 Bertrand Russell, 'On Denoting', in *Logic and Knowledge*, ed. Robert C. Marsh, London, Allen and Unwin, 1956, p. 54.
11 A much better objection against the argument is the very compressed argument given by St Thomas Aquinas in *Summa Theologica*, trans. Fathers of the English Dominican Province, Ottawa, Collège Dominicain d' Ottawa, 1941, First Part, Q2, Art. 2, Reply Obj. 2. What may very well be the same argument is given by Russell as a consequence of the theory of descriptions in 'On Denoting', p. 54.

Reading

St Anselm, *The Prayers and Meditations of St Anselm, with the Proslogion*, ed. Sister Benedicta Ward, Harmondsworth, Penguin, 1973.
Jonathan Barnes, *The Ontological Argument*, London, Macmillan, 1972.
W.E. Mann, 'The Perfect Island', *Mind* lxxxv, No. 339 (1976), pp. 417–421.
*Alvin Plantinga, ed., *The Ontological Argument from St Anselm to Contemporary Philosophers*, New York, Doubleday, 1965.
C.J.F. Williams, *What is Existence?* Oxford, Oxford University Press, 1981.

5
Certainty
What Is Certainty and What Is Certain?

A
Background

It is natural for people to want to be certain of things, and not just the theological things discussed in the last chapter. Uncertainty about anything can be very uncomfortable. It is an uncomfortable feeling not to be certain whether the car will make it the last thirty miles home on the petrol in the tank – uncomfortable, that is, if one does not have the money to buy more, or if there is nowhere to buy it from. (Some people find situations like this one exciting, but these people have other problems. They are the kind of people who climb mountains and leap unprovoked out of aeroplanes. Perhaps, though, part of the legitimate exhilaration and challenge of these activities is achieving certainty and control over great danger.) And so it is natural to want to know in advance, in a general way, of what one can be certain. If I am not entitled under any circumstances to feel certain about how much petrol is in the tank, because I cannot *see* how much there is, and this for the general philosophical reason that I can only be certain about what I can see, then I ought in consistency to feel uncomfortable about making it home even when I have just filled the tank. So I ought to feel uncomfortable all the time about everything I cannot see. Is this right?

The question of what I can be certain of can also arise from the confusion caused by competing claims to knowledge and the apparently competing claims of faith. If I am not entitled to feel certain about the truth of evolution, say, then that may have an effect on the certainty of my religious views. Or it may not. The degree and kind of certainty one feels about religious matters can also influence what one thinks about matters which are at least partly scientific, such as the origin of the universe.

In matters of unadulterated science, though, as well as in theology and religion, contradictory claims are also regularly advanced. The mechanism of evolution is natural selection alone; the mechanism of evolution is not natural selection alone. The universe is eight billion years old; the universe is fifteen billion years old.

In religion and philosophical theology, the philosophical situation is harder because the evidence and the arguments are not as direct and involve religious faith. We say that God exists, or that God does not exist. God loves us; God has abandoned us. One way of trying to sort out the truth of such claims is to ask what one thinks one can be certain of. Having answered that, the next step is to ask what, if anything, justifies the certainty.

The importance of questions about certainty in modern philosophy is due to the pivotal role which they played in the philosophy of Descartes. Before Descartes, as Ernest Gellner, a sociologist and maverick philosopher, observed, 'knowledge is *something in the world*'. After the time of Descartes, he said, 'the world becomes *something in knowledge*'.[1] He meant that with Descartes every proposition had to be fully justified to be counted as certain knowledge.

Descartes believed that initially he could only be certain in his sense of his own subjective states of consciousness. He might not be certain that what he heard was a skylark singing, but he was certain that he was aware of a certain sort of undescribed sound. He might not be certain that the world external to him existed, but he was certain that he himself existed, as this was a precondition for even doubting his own existence.

Descartes' 'quest for certainty', as it has been called, set the programme for much of the subsequent history of philosophy. The primary question was *how* one could advance with certainty beyond one's own subjective states. There was also the question of how *far* one could advance, if at all, and with what justification. Descartes' model for certainty was the clarity and distinctness with which he apprehended, or thought he did, his own subjective states, and with which he apprehended mathematical truths. Here he was the heir to an historical tradition of thought coming down from Plato, which gave the highest certainty to mathematics.

B
Knowledge of Eternal Truth

In Plato's metaphysics, reality consists of perfect and unchanging templates or Forms of things, such as 'the beautiful itself', which 'inform'[2] all the many 'beautiful things'.[3] Certainty then consists of the apprehension of these Forms. Since the Forms 'are always the same in every respect',[4] once we apprehend them, we apprehend something which cannot change. We can be certain of knowledge of the Forms, because unlike 'opinion' it never lies, and it is always of what is.[5] Sensory and empirical knowledge are not certain, because they are not eternally true. 'Here today, gone tomorrow' is the motto of an untrustworthy character. Certainty is eternal truth. One cannot be certain of the changing empirical world delivered by the senses. Mathematics, for example the knowledge that the interior angles of the triangle are the same as two right angles, or that the triangle has three sides, is the paradigm of certainty for Plato. As philosophers would say today, according to Plato these truths are (1) 'a priori' and (2) 'necessary'.

(1) By an *a priori* truth is meant one which we know independently of experience of 'the many . . . things', which are empirical instances, such as the many beautiful things. We know *a priori* that all bachelors are unmarried men, to take a hackneyed example, because we know it independently of any statistical survey of the marital status and sex of bachelors. The opposite of '*a priori*' is 'empirical' or '*a posteriori*'.

(2) By a necessary truth is meant a truth which cannot be false. It is obviously and necessarily true that a triangle must have exactly three sides, and this is because ('join up the dots') it is a closed figure with three angles. Compare this with the truth, assuming it is one, 'It is raining in London.' This has seemed to many living in London to be almost a necessary truth, but sometimes it is not raining in London. Yet if 'It is raining in London' is a truth, it is a *contingent* truth. One has, one way or another, to find out what the London weather is doing to determine its truth or falsity. For Plato, however:

> It is certain that $7 \times 9 = 63$.
> ↓
> It is eternally true that $7 \times 9 = 63$.

Plato's analysis of certainty as eternal truth has the consequence that we cannot be certain that there is petrol in the tank, even when we know, or think that we do, that we have just filled it. For true knowledge is not of this tank of petrol, but of eternal Forms of things. Consider an example of a truth which is neither known *a priori* nor is necessary, and suppose it is certain.

> It is certain that Jonathan Westphal is wearing blue pyjamas now.
> ↓

It is eternally true that Jonathan Westphal is wearing blue pyjamas now.

There is much to think about here. Perhaps it is eternally true, as it were from now on, that what the proposition says *was* true. After all, it is not going to become false that at the time the proposition was uttered Jonathan Westphal *was* wearing blue pyjamas. But of course the proposition does not say that he *was* wearing blue pyjamas now, but that he is. And this proposition, if it is taken to mean that Jonathan Westphal is *always* wearing blue pyjamas, and if that in turn is taken to mean that we know or he knows *a priori* that he is wearing blue pyjamas, and if that means that it is necessarily true that he is wearing blue pyjamas, is false. Taken this way, if Plato's analysis is correct, the given proposition is *false*.

This is a serious puzzle for Plato, having indeed the force of a counterexample. It does, however, suppose or make the assumption that I *can* be certain that I am wearing blue pyjamas, because I can see them, or that there is petrol in the tank, because I just filled it. The criticism of Plato is that 'I'm certain that I am wearing blue pyjamas, because I can see them' and 'I'm certain the tank is full, because I just filled it, and because the gauge shows full' are not *necessarily* false. But for Plato I can only be of the *opinion* that I am wearing blue pyjamas or that I have just filled the tank. Our attachment to such truths derives from the senses and the memory, not from the 'infallible' knowledge of a Form.[6]

Yet Plato's arguments for the fallibility of our 'non-Formal' knowledge are not easy to disentangle. He likens knowledge of 'what is', of 'the beautiful itself' or 'the triangle itself', triangularity, to being awake, and the belief of someone who believes only in the many beautiful things or the many triangles to *dreaming*. 'Isn't this dreaming: whether asleep or awake, to think that a likeness is not a likeness but rather the thing itself that it is like?'[7] This definition of dreaming is too broad, as it makes a case of mistakenly thinking I see a friend on the street, from the back, into 'living in a dream rather than in a wakened state'.[8] It is surely rather a case of both (a) being awake *and* (b) being mistaken, i.e., believing something false, not of dreaming at all.

One of Plato's mistakes was to confuse the proposition that making a mistake is a kind of dream, which is false, with the proposition that a dream is a kind of mistake-making, which is, in a minimal sense, true. The sense in which the latter proposition is true is simply that if I dream that I live in Alaska, though I really live in Idaho, then for all that what I dream is not true. For this to amount to a positive mistake, however, requires that I actually *believe* the dream. And not all dreams involve beliefs that what is going on in the dream is actually going on.

A final note is in order here. The primary question of what we can be certain of invites consideration of the logically prior question of what certainty is. 'Logically prior' is opposed here to 'temporally prior' or 'prior in the order of investigation or of being answered'. We might ask the question of what things we can be certain of before asking the logically prior question of what certainty is. Then we would work out the analysis of what certainty is on the basis of the analysis of cases which have antecedently been decided to be cases of certainty. Neither order is essential, though. We could start with cases which we think are cases of certainty, and try to arrive at an analysis of certainty by generalizing from them. Or we could start with the analysis of certainty and assess alleged cases of certainty on the basis of the analysis. Or we could try to do both at once. We started with the analysis given by Plato, but we could equally well have started with his argument that particular cases of empirical truth are never certain; for example, the truth that there is enough petrol in the tank to get home. Plato's answers to the two questions of what certainty is and what we can be certain of are two sides of the same coin. Since certainty is eternity, the only truths we can be certain of are eternal.

Let us consider another analysis, this time a medieval one.

C
Freedom from Doubt

St Thomas Aquinas distinguishes two senses in which a thing may be certain.

1 A thing, he says, may be certain 'on the part of its cause, and thus a thing which has a more certain cause, is itself more certain'.[9] In this sense, religious faith is more certain than reason and science, because it proceeds from something which, St Thomas says, is more certain than they are, namely 'divine truth'.

2 Certainty may also be 'considered on the part of [=relative to] the subject, and thus the more a man lays hold of a thing, the more certain it is'. In this sense, science and reason and the two other 'intellectual virtues' (wisdom and understanding) are more certain than the truths of faith.

Here, perhaps, is the distinction between two forms of certainty: (a) 'It is certain that p'; and (b) 'I am certain that p.' St Thomas would agree with Plato that the proposition that it is certain that Jonathan Westphal is wearing blue pyjamas is false, but he would distinguish it from:

I am certain that Jonathan Westphal is wearing blue pyjamas
now.
↓
I have no doubt that Jonathan Westphal is wearing blue
pyjamas now.

How then would St Thomas understand or analyse the proposition that
it is certain that something is the case? Clearly he would want to retain a
connection between his 'two ways of looking' at certainty. So it is natural
to interpret him to mean that the certainty which is looked at in the two
different ways, from the point of view of the subject and from the point of
view of the subject matter, is the same, or that 'certainty' has the same
sense in the (a) and (b) formulations. Then for him:

It is certain that Jonathan Westphal is wearing blue pyjamas
now.
↓
There is no doubt that Jonathan Westphal is wearing blue
pyjamas now.

St Thomas' analysis is a good deal more plausible than Plato's, because
it is less vulnerable to counterexamples. Yet there is a problem. Consider
again:

It is certain that $7 \times 9 = 63$.
↓
There is no doubt that $7 \times 9 = 63$.

Yet what if there is a doubt in my mind, or in the mind of a schoolgirl
struggling to learn her 9-times table? 'Is $7 \times 9 = 63$?' she asks uneasily.

Or was it 62? But then 6×9 was 54, and so, by the rule of
subtracting one from the unit column and adding one to the ten
– but was that the rule? Or was it the other way around? . . .
um, perhaps the answer *isn't* 63.

There may be doubts in the minds of people about propositions about
which there should really be no doubt at all. A person suffering from
paranoia may doubt the benign intentions of those around him or
her, when there *should* be no doubt, and when, in this sense, there *is* no
doubt.

The paranoia case demands a further analysis of the mathematical
propositions. We can go on from:

There is no doubt that $7 \times 9 = 63$.
↓
There is no *reasonable* doubt that $7 \times 9 = 63$.

This proposition means that if there are doubts, they are not reasonable.

This of course does raise the question of what a reasonable doubt is, and, if it should be answered that it is the doubt of a reasonable person, what exactly a reasonable person is. No doubt even reasonable people are not reasonable all the time. In practical matters, though, where certainty is very important, if it is available, for example in serious legal matters or in matters of military intelligence, a reasonable person is one who is guided by the available reasons for the truth or falsity of a proposition and not by something else; in short, who is guided by the evidence. A reasonable person is one whose beliefs are sensitive to the reasons available, or at least the ones given, for the truth of a proposition. An unreasonable person may believe that her or his friends wish to destroy her or him, in the absence of any reasons. A reasonable person will want to allow her or his beliefs to be sensitive to the evidence available to her or him.

The formulation of the analysis of 'reasonable' in terms of *reasons* is preferable to the formulation in terms of *evidence*, because there are some propositions, e.g. those of metaphysics, if any, or mathematics, where there are better and worse arguments, better and worse reasons, but these reasons do not have the character, exactly, of evidence.

The schoolgirl actually does have a reasonable doubt, from her own point of view. Or is it simply that she doesn't know the answer? She is in doubt about what the answer is, and she *thinks* it may be 63, but she isn't sure. Her doubts about 63 would be paralleled by doubts about any number not too far from it, e.g. 62 and 64. The degree of her competence in arithmetic will be a measure of how wide this band of doubt is. In her case, it is not very wide. She almost has the answer. But she is not yet completely competent in arithmetic, and she is not qualified to judge the answers to even more difficult questions, such as (horrors!) what 8×9 is, or even 13×17.

The proposition that I am wearing blue pyjamas is certain, because I have the strongest possible reason for thinking that I am wearing blue pyjamas, namely, that I am *looking right at them*. Is this enough, though? Mightn't I be dreaming? If the proposition is certain, however, it is because the 'evidence' of my eyes could not be improved upon, that is, that there could not be a better reason than this, that I can *see* the colour of my pyjamas. A person competent to judge this question requires just one skill or ability, namely normal eyesight, as compared with the rather complex acquired skills of the judge and the arithmetician.

Reasonable doubt, then, should be understood as the doubt of a reasonable person (the schoolgirl is not *un*reasonable, like the paranoid), who is *competent* or qualified to judge, or who is, in *this* sense, able to judge, as opposed merely to guessing.

With the detour through the concept of a reasonable *person*, the analysis of the proposition that it is certain that $7 \times 9 = 63$ would come down to the proposition that there is no reason to doubt that $7 \times 9 = 63$. Yet the claim being made in the original proposition is a little stronger than this. It is not even just that there is no reason available to reasonable persons, such as we of course are, but that there *could* be no such reason. We shall come back to this view. It goes well beyond St Thomas' own discussion, though in a direction which is consistent with his discussion and which he might have found congenial.

As a preparation for this, let us note that St Thomas' analysis is not sufficient or complete. Plainly there are things which are not in doubt, but which are not certain. Mere *absence* of doubt does not imply certainty. Suppose for example that the number of stars is some vast but definite number S. No one doubts that S is the number of the stars, because no one has ever thought of the number S before, and therefore has entertained the thought that it is the number of the stars. Yet it is not true that anyone is certain that 'The number of stars is S', or that this is certain or a certain truth. Why not? What is missing from St Thomas' analysis?

D
Indubitability

Descartes uses, in his *Meditations*,[10] a more demanding conception of certainty than St Thomas'. St Thomas gives the absence of doubt as the analysis of certainty. Descartes gives not merely the absence but the *impossibility* of doubt, indubitability, as the analysis. What cannot be doubted is certain. Descartes' method of discovering certain truths was to subject all propositions to doubt. Those which survived the doubt would be *indubitable*, incapable of being doubted. This was the basis of their certainty, and their justification as knowledge. The first result of Descartes' method was the so-called *cogito* (Latin for 'I think'), which is the tag for *cogito ergo sum*, 'I think therefore I am.'

> And observing that this truth – *I am thinking, therefore I exist* – was so firm and sure that the most extravagant suppositions of the sceptics were incapable of shaking it, I decided that I could accept it without scruple as the first principle of the philosophy I was seeking.[11]

From the way in which the *cogito* gains its certainty and truth, Descartes deduced what has been called 'the truth rule':[12] 'the things we conceive very clearly and very distinctly are all true'.[13] For these things are all certain, in Descartes' sense (of indubitability), and the truth rule converts certainties into truths.

Clearly and distinctly perceived ↔ Indubitable ↔ Certain →
True

The central equations here, of clarity and distinctness with indubitability, and of indubitability with certainty, give Descartes his analysis of what certainty is, as well as his answer to the question which truths are certain in the given sense. They could be formulated as an argument consisting of two hypothetical syllogisms, ending up with the conclusion that whatever is clearly and distinctly perceived is true. Taking the second syllogism:

I am certain that $7 \times 9 = 63$.
↓
I cannot doubt that $7 \times 9 = 63$.

Which propositions or truths cannot be doubted? Descartes' answer is that only clearly and distinctly perceived things are indubitable. Mathematics is one example of clarity and distinctness. Another is our own conscious states. I may not be certain that what I am seeing actually is a pair of blue pyjamas because, according to Descartes, for all I know I am dreaming. But even if I am dreaming, I am having a conscious experience of the image of a pair of blue pyjamas. This is what I seem to see, and I cannot doubt that I seem to see it.

This raises the question of exactly what Descartes means by clear and distinct perception, and this has vexed commentators on his philosophy. In No. 45 of Part I of a work called *The Principles of Philosophy*,[14] he characterizes a clear proposition or judgement as one which is fully present to the mind contemplating it, a sense which Descartes likens to seeing things clearly with the eyes. It is distinct if it is so precisely distinguished from other propositions or judgements as to be completely clear. Then, Descartes thinks, the proposition is indubitable.

What this comes to is that clarity is the foundation of certainty, and that certainty is a function of clarity.

p is certain.
↓
p is clear.

Yet this cannot be right.[15] It may seem to be right in pure mathematics, a field in which Descartes was a genius, and in which truth does not involve in any obvious way a correspondence to facts. There are no *a posteriori* truths in mathematics. Yet there are *a posteriori* truths which are completely clear, but which are not certain. For example, the proposition that there are more than seventeen books of over 100 pages in my room at the moment is a perfectly clear one. I can easily doubt it, though. And I will not be certain that it is true unless I go and count the books. Then my certainty has the clarity of the proposition as a precondition, but what is actually producing the certainty is counting the books, or checking the proposition against the fact.

E
Knowledge Plus an Unimprovably Good Justification

It is time for some puzzles. In epistemology, the study or theory of knowledge, which is what we are discussing, they are not hard to find. Here are two.

> The Puzzle of Certainty Under Change
> How can we be certain of anything? Nothing will necessarily stay the same, and so what we feel certain of can always let us down. There is always room for doubt.

We have already resolved this problem. It is not too hard to get the measure of it once one has seen that there is nothing necessary about Plato's analysis of certainty as eternal truth. The puzzle of certainty under change merely *assumes* that if a proposition is not eternally true or necessary, it cannot be certain. But, as we saw, there is no particular reason to think that this is so, especially as it makes all empirical truths uncertain. It might seem as if necessary truths are certain in Descartes' sense. Yet they are, in a psychological sense, no more indubitable than any other propositions.

> The Regress Puzzle
> How can we be certain of anything? A proposition p derives its certainty from another proposition q which supports it. Let p be the proposition that $12^3 = 1,728$. This is a certainty, but only so

because of a number of other propositions, including the proposition – call it q – that $2 \times 4 = 8$. The calculation of the cube of 12 involves multiplying 144 by 12, and the first step of this multiplication is q: 2×4. Then the same logic applies to q. So either (1) *emergence*: q is itself not certain. Or (2) *regress*: p derives its certainty from q, q derives its certainty from r, and this goes on forever. (Here is the regress.) Or (3) *circularity*: p derives its certainty from q, q derives its certainty from r, and r derives its certainty from p. Or (4) *non-implication*: the certainty of p does not derive from any other proposition.[16]

Options (2) and (3) in the regress puzzle may be dismissed on logical grounds. (4) will require an analysis of certainty which bestows it on propositions in virtue of some intrinsic feature, such as necessity or indubitability. This has been called 'foundationalism'. The idea is that some propositions are *basic*, and their certainty does not derive from other propositions: 'The buck stops here.' We have seen some difficulties with this type of analysis with Plato and Descartes. That leaves (1) *emergence*. Here is the analysis of certainty which I think is correct, and which solves the regress problem.

S is certain that p.
↓
S knows that p, and the justification which S has for the belief that p is *unimprovably good*.

It is a positive virtue of this analysis that it can very easily be formulated for both of the forms 'I/a subject S am/is certain . . .' and the impersonal 'It is certain . . .'.

It is certain that p.
↓
It is known that p, and the justification for the belief that p is *unimprovably good*.

The inclusion of knowledge in certainty is the extra condition which St Thomas missed. Or perhaps he simply assumed it. If S is certain of p, then S knows p. Some things we know, however, are not derived from an unimprovable justification. S says, for example, that she knows what time it is because she has just been told the time by someone with a reliable and expensive watch. Though it does not surely affect whether S does have knowledge in the first place, one can imagine in this particular case that the justification of such knowledge could be improved, by even more corroborating evidence.

It is perhaps significant that the propositions using the two forms of certainty imply Aquinas' condition that there is no doubt about p, but in the normative sense that there really *should* or *ought* to be no doubt.

The analyis of certainty as an unimprovably good justification implies that whatever is known can be known for certain, and also implies that what is known can be certain. So if I can know what time it is, or if I can know that it is about to rain, or what the structure of DNA is, or that a child is suffering from neglect and malnutrition, then I can be certain of these truths, by the analysis, or they can be certain. If I am asked, 'Is it (or was it) certain that the child was suffering from neglect and malnutrition?', I can then answer, with complete confidence and truth, 'Yes.' The justification of this statement will be the demonstration that the justification of the original statement was unimprovably good, that the evidence for the truth of the proposition was perfectly adequate and unimprovably so.

This analysis, in the personal form, requires that nothing could show that the justification S has for p could be any better. An evidential consideration cannot be produced which would or should make S want to say, 'Now my justification has been *improved*', because it is already as good as it can get. The arguments of sceptics which impress philosophers like Descartes, however, are directed towards showing there is always a consideration which could or should make S want to say, 'Now my justification has been *dis*improved.' According to these philosophers, S's justification for thinking that p ('the cat is sitting on the mat'), which is that S is himself sitting on the mat, stroking the cat, and can see the cat on the mat beside him, is no good, because he might be dreaming that he can see the cat sitting on the mat. So S is or should not be not certain that p. What these philosophers have shown, however, is not that S's justification cannot be *strengthened* by the addition of additional truths (such as q, that 'S reads in the newspaper that the cat is sitting on the mat') but, negatively, that the justification for S's belief that p is one which can be *weakened* if it can be shown that certain propositions other than p are or may be true, for example r, that S is dreaming. If the unimprovability analysis is correct, this is irrelevant. It is the lack of possible improvement in the justification, by the addition of further truths, which makes for certainty, not the lack of a possible disimprovement. Descartes apparently did not appreciate this distinction.

The word 'certain' comes from the Latin *cernere*, to sift, to discern, to decide. It shares one sense with 'sure', said of things which are fixed or secure, or not going to *move* or change, like boats which are made 'secure'. What is 'sure' is therefore 'safe from danger or harm'. The epistemological danger is of course not from wind and tide, but from falsehood. The present analysis says that if a justification for p is unimprovably good, then the claim that p is secure in the sense that p is not going to change its truth-value from true to false.

How does this analysis solve the regress puzzle? Suppose I am certain that p, and that my certainty that p derives from q. The analyses do not tell us that the justification of p, which is q, has *itself* to be certain. All that is required is that it should be unimprovably good, which is not quite the same thing. Certainty then emerges from two conditions.

1   p is known, either by S or by enough people to justify the application of the phrase 'it is known', so that p is common knowledge.

2   The justification of p, which we are calling q, is unimprovably good.

The significance of the second condition is that if the justification could be improved on, then it could also be the case that it was *not* improved on. In that case the absence of the possible improvement would allow a doubt to suggest itself. Then p would not be certain after all, at least in Descartes' sense and in St Thomas'.

The second condition of the analysis of certainty says that S is in the best possible position, in terms of justification, to know p, or could not be in a better one. An obvious example of this is the certainty of someone fully sighted looking at the blue pyjamas he is wearing and considering the proposition that he is wearing blue pyjamas. His epistemic (= knowledge-related) position could not be improved upon, and no amount of further evidence or argument could add to his certainty, nor should it. He is certain that he is wearing blue pyjamas, we say, because he knows it, and his evidence, the justification for his belief, is that he can see the blue pyjamas, and that he is wearing them, with his own eyes.

Another example: I know for certain that p, '$12^3 = 1,728$'. What justifies this truth and makes it certain is, among other propositions, q, which says that $2 \times 4 = 8$. What makes q certain, though? Well, whatever the answer to *this* question, all that is required for the certainty of p is surely that q, and the other propositions involved in the multiplication, are *known*, not that they are themselves known with perfect certainty. (In this example, however, there is a strong case for thinking that this extra and unnecessary condition is also satisfied.) Knowledge, on this view, does not imply certainty, because it does not imply the possession or even the existence of the perfect justification.

Some more examples. I am certain that

	p:	I am 47 years old,
because		I know p,
and	q:	I know that I was born in 1951 and that it is now 1998.

Here q could not be bettered as a justification. One could invent cases in which the evidence that S has for her own birthdate is less good than the evidence some official person has, and further that S is actually mistaken about the year of her birth as a result. This would weaken the confidence one has in claims to know propositions like q. But this does not apply for most of us in ordinary middle-class circumstances, with the whole apparatus of birthdays and passport applications, driving licences and more or less accurate oral family history from the previous generation.

It is worth noticing that without the 'I know' in q, q doesn't follow from p. 'I was born in 1951' does *not* imply that 'I am certain that I am 47 years old.' Another example. I am certain that

	p:	My cat is called Fuffy,
because		I know p,
and	q:	I named her myself.

Here again, it is hard to see how there could be a better justification for p than q. And since q is a perfect justification for p, and I know that p, according to the proposed analysis, I am certain that p.

The proposition that S is certain that p is nicely ambiguous, as G.E. Moore pointed out, hovering between 'S *feels* certain that p' and 'S *knows for* certain that p.' We can say, for example, 'I was certain that I had left my watch in the bathroom, but I found it on the bedside table.' What is meant here may be that I merely felt certain, and that if I was certain, I should not have been. In 'Certainty' Moore distinguishes 'S feels certain that p', 'S is certain that p', 'S knows for certain that p' and 'It is certain that p.'[17] The present analysis gives an easy way to construe 'S feels certain that p.' What this means is that S believes or is confident, rightly or wrongly, that S knows that p, and also that he *knows* that the justification for p which he has could not be improved on. The point is that he may be wrong. But he may also be right. 'Feeling certain' *may* then be a matter of an intuitive sense or a strong conviction, but it may also simply be the detached belief that one is certain. What converts feeling certain into being certain is unimprovably good evidence. If in addition one knows that one has such evidence, then one is justified in claiming to know for certain, as opposed simply to knowing. This in turn gives one the *right* to feel certain. Thus being certain is feeling certain, and having the right to it.

Historical Note

The driving interest in certainty, the 'quest for certainty', as the American philosopher John Dewey called it, began with Descartes in the seventeenth century. Descartes made the theory of knowledge the leading department of philosophy. This emphasis lasted until the re-emergence of logic at the centre of philosophy in the twentieth century, and the theory of knowledge was displaced by the logic of concepts, in the work of Wittgenstein and the English linguistic philosophers, and by a conception of philosophy as continuous with science, in the work of Quine in America. Though scepticism is now widely believed to have been refuted, there is very little consensus on where certainty is to be found, if anywhere.

Notes

1 Ernest Gellner, 'Philosophy: The Social Context', in Bryan Magee, *Men of Ideas*, Oxford, Oxford University Press, 1982, p. 253.
2 A metaphor which actually comes to us from Plato.
3 Plato, *The Republic*, trans. G.M.A. Grube, Indianapolis/Cambridge, Mass., Hackett, 1992, Book V, p. 151.
4 Ibid., p. 156.
5 Ibid., p. 153.
6 Ibid.
7 Ibid., p. 151.
8 Ibid.
9 St Thomas Aquinas, 'Whether Faith is More Certain than Science and the Other Intellectual Virtues?', in *Summa Theologica*, trans. Fathers of the English Dominican Province, Ottawa, Collège Dominicain d'Ottawa, 1941, Part II of Second Part, Q4, Art. 8.
10 René Descartes, 'Meditations On First Philosophy', in *The Philosophical Writings of Descartes*, Vol. II, trans. and ed. John Cottingham, Robert Stoothof and Dugald Murdoch, Cambridge, Cambridge University Press, 1984, pp. 13–14.
11 Descartes, *Discourse on the Method*, in *Philosophical Writings*, Vol. I, p. 127.
12 Louis E. Loeb, 'The Cartesian Circle', in John Cottingham, ed., *The Cambridge Companion to Descartes*, Cambridge, Cambridge University Press, 1992, p. 200.
13 Descartes, *Philosophical Writings*, Vol. I, p. 127.
14 Ibid., pp. 207–208.
15 According to Russell Wahl, it also cannot be Descartes. Descartes, Wahl has said in conversation, gave the truth rule as a rule about clear and distinct *perceptions*, not about propositions, and the truth which it yielded was not propositional truth but something more like the acquaintance with a Platonic rational essence.
16 This problem is stated in terms of the *certainty* of propositions, rather than, as it usually is in epistemology, in terms of the *justification* of *beliefs*. Aristotle's original version, in the 'Posterior Analytics' (in Jonathan Barnes, ed., *The Complete Works of Aristotle*, Princeton, Princeton Univeristy Press, 1984, Vol. 1, p. 117) discusses regress,

circularity and non-implication in terms of that without which there would not be *understanding*. Ludwig Wittgenstein's compelling solution, which uses the distinction between actual and possible infinite series, is found in *The Blue and Brown Books*, Oxford, Blackwell, 1958, pp. 14–15.

17 G.E. Moore, 'Certainty', in *Philosophical Papers*, London, Allen and Unwin, 1959, p. 238.

Reading

A.J. Ayer, *The Problem of Knowledge*, Harmondsworth, Penguin, 1956, esp. Ch. 2, 'Scepticism and Certainty'.

Jonathan Dancy, *Introduction to Contemporary Epistemology*, Oxford, Blackwell, 1985.

Stephen Cade Hetherington, *Knowledge Puzzles: An Introduction to Epistemology*, Boulder, Colo., Westview, 1996.

G.E. Moore, 'A Defence of Common Sense' and 'Proof of an External World', in *Philosophical Papers*, London, Allen and Unwin, 1959.

C.D. Rollins, 'Certainty', in *The Encyclopedia of Philosophy*, ed. Paul Edwards, Vol. I, New York, Macmillan, 1967.

*Jonathan Westphal, ed., *Certainty*, Indianapolis, Ind./Cambridge, Mass., Hackett, 1995.

Ludwig Wittgenstein, *On Certainty*, ed. G.E.M. Anscombe and G.H. von Wright, Oxford, Blackwell, 1969.

6
Time
How Can Time Exist?

A
The Puzzles

Time has seemed profoundly puzzling to many philosophers, from the early Greeks to the modern linguistic philosophers. There seem to have been two aspects of time which together have invited philosophical wonderment.

1   Time is invisible, and also intangible and in general *non-sensory*.

2   Yet time *moves*, apparently detectably, because its passage can be measured.

Many things are invisible, of course, and many things move. So the difficulties about time lie deeper. They come to the surface in one large question.

3   How can such a queer thing as time *exist* and be measured?

The questions are related, of course. The philosophical wonder about the existence of time really concerns the relationship between points 1 and 2. How can something non-sensory *move*? How can something *exist* which is non-sensory? What sort of existence is this? How can something non-sensory be *measured* or otherwise *detected*? How can it be measured by such definitely sensory things as clocks?

Well-formulated puzzles can serve to make this kind of vague puzzlement precise.

The Puzzle of the Unreality of Time
To start, then: the following considerations would make one suspect that it [time] does not exist or only barely, and in an obscure way. One part of it has been and is not, while the other part is going to be and is not yet. Yet time – both infinite time and any time you care to mention – is made up of these. One would naturally suppose that what is made up of things which do not exist could have no share in reality.[1]

St Augustine, the fourth- and fifth-century church father and Christian philosopher, states the same puzzle in Chapter XIV of Book Eleven of the *Confessions*.[2] 'But the two times, past and future, how can they *be*, since the past is no more and the future is not yet?'

There is a further problem which St Augustine thinks is a consequence, having to do with the *length* of the past.

The Puzzle of the Properties of the Past
If we say the past was long, was it long when it was already past or while it was still present? It could be long only while it was in existence to *be* long. But the past no longer exists. It cannot be long, because it is not at all.

This leads St Augustine to consider the possibility that a long past time was long when it was present, because, after all, when it was present it hadn't yet disappeared into the past, 'though once it passed away, it ceased to be long by ceasing to be'. This puzzle may seem to involve a certain amount of confusion about tenses, but the question at which St Augustine arrives as a result embodies a real problem which takes off from the question of whether the present can be long or have any length at all.

The Puzzle of the Retrenchability of the Present
Are the present hundred years a long time? But first see whether a hundred years *can* be present. If it is the first year of the hundred, then that year is present, but the other ninety-nine are still in the future, and so as yet are not: if we are in the second year, then one year is past, one year is present, the rest future. Thus whichever year of our hundred-year period we choose as present, those before it have passed away, those after it are still to come. Thus a hundred years cannot be present.

But now let us see if the chosen year is itself present. If we are in the first month, the others are still to come, if in the second, the first has passed away and the rest are not yet. Thus if a year is not wholly present, then the year is not present. For a year is twelve months, and the month that happens to be running its course is the only one present, the others either are no longer or as yet are not. Even the current month is not present, but only one day of it: if that day is the first, the rest are still to come; if the last, the rest are passed away; if somewhere between, it has days past on one side and days still to come on the other.

Thus the present, which we have found to be the only time capable of being long, is cut down to the space of barely one day. But if we examine this one day, even it is not wholly present. A day is composed of twenty-four hours – day-hours, night-hours: the first hour finds the rest still to come, the last hour finds the rest passed away, any hour between has hours passed before it, hours to come after it. And that one hour is made of fleeing moments: so much of the hour as has fled away is the past, what still remains is the future. If we conceive of some point of time which cannot be divided into even the minutest parts of moments, that is the only point that can be called present: and that point flees at such lightning speed from being future to being past, that it has no duration at all. For if it were so extended, it would be divisible into past and future: the present has no length.[3]

If the present has no length, how then can anything happen *in* the present? If I claim to have a bath so narrow as to have no width, how can I expect anybody to believe that there is anything *in* it, or could be anything in it, even the tiniest little yellow rubber bath ducky?

The Puzzle of the Non-existence of the Present
If the present has no length, how can any changes take place in it? Then since by the puzzle of Time's Unreality the past and the future also do not exist for changes to take place in, there can be no changes. But there obviously can be changes, since there are changes.
   If the present does not have length, how can all of it *be* present (by the argument in the puzzle of the retrenchability of the present)?

There are more related puzzles of equal interest. An important one in the history of ideas is the following, because it relates Aristotle's discussion in the *Physics* to St Augustine's *Confessions*, and through them to Wittgenstein's *Blue Book*.

The Impossibility of Measuring Time
'How do we measure time present, since it has no extent [= duration, length]? It is measured while it is passing; once it has passed, it cannot be measured, for then nothing exists to measure.'[4] Yet this will not do, for even if the present is moving, if it has no length it cannot be measured.

B
Wittgenstein's Resolution of St Augustine's Puzzle

St Augustine's own solution to these problems is inadequate. His solution is a psychological one, and this does not clear up the logical difficulties of the problem, and in addition it creates logical difficulties of its own. His solution is that since time cannot be measured in reality, as it has no length or duration:

It is in you, O my mind, that I measure time . . . What I measure is the impress produced in you by things as they pass and abiding in you when they have passed: and it is present. I do not measure the things themselves whose passage produced the impress; it is the impress that I measure when I measure time. Thus either that is what time is, or I am not measuring time.[5]

So we cannot say that it took half an hour to eat lunch, for then, St Augustine thinks, we would be stuck with the question of how the present, or the past, could be so long as to take half an hour! If lunch was eaten in the present, as he conceives it, it took no time, and if it was eaten in the past, it was not eaten, as the past does not exist.

What takes half an hour, he thinks, is the *experience* of eating lunch, which is preserved in memory. And what is measured is the memory.

This seems confused. The memory of a half-hour lunch certainly does not last half an hour, in spite of St Augustine's claim that 'a long past is merely a long memory of the past'[6] (which seems to imply that the past could be destroyed by destroying the memory of the past) and his even more obviously untrue claim that 'it is not the future that is long, for the future does not exist: a long future is merely a long expectation of the future.' Does it take a whole summer to expect next summer? And the difference between a man who will live another fifty years and a man who has only a day to live is, according to St Augustine, that we *expect* the former to live longer!

According to Wittgenstein, what is behind puzzlements such as St Augustine's 'puzzlement about the grammar of the word "time"' is 'what one might call apparent contradictions in that grammar'.[7] Wittgenstein's summary of St Augustine's problem runs together two or more of the puzzles given above.

> How is it possible that one should measure time? For the past can't be measured, as it is gone by; and the future can't be measured because it has not yet come. And the present can't be measured for it has no extension.[8]

What does Wittgenstein mean by an 'apparent contradiction in [the] grammar' of the word 'time'? He says that 'The man who is philosophically puzzled sees a law in the way a word is used, and trying to apply the law consistently, comes up against cases where it leads to paradoxical results.'[9]

Here is a 'law' which seems to fit Wittgenstein's meaning.

> Aristotle's Rule
> In order to measure the length of something, say the length of X, all parts of X must be present simultaneously or at the same time. For example, to measure something which is six inches long with a twelve-inch ruler, the whole of the six-inch length must be present at the same time.[10]

This seems reasonable. Now let us apply this 'law' or rule to a case where it leads to a 'paradoxical result'. Let X itself be a time, say a year. Our task is to measure the year. Applying Aristotle's Rule, we get:

> In order to measure X (a year) all parts of X (a year) must be present *at the same time*. But a year is a time. So in order to measure a time, all parts of the time must be present *at the same time*.

So applied, Aristotle's Rule seems to be contradictory. By the Rule the whole year must be present at the same time to be present at all! The whole of the year must be squashed into the present. And this is what St Augustine thinks is impossible, since only one month of the year can be present, and of this month only one day, and so on.

The contradiction which here seems to arise could be called a conflict between two different usages of a word, in this case the word 'measure'. Augustine, we might say, thinks of the process of measuring a length: say, the distance between two marks on a travelling band which passes us, and of which we see only a tiny bit (the present) in front of us. Solving this puzzle will consist in comparing what we mean by 'measurement' (the grammar of the word 'measurement') when applied to a distance on a travelling band with the grammar of that word when applied to time. The problem may seem simple, but its extreme difficulty is due to the fascination which the analogy between two similar structures in language can exert on us. (It is helpful here to remember that it is sometimes almost impossible for a child to believe that one word can have two meanings.)[11]

The part of the travelling band between the two marks which is to be measured, like time, is never all present at once in the 'tiny bit' in front of us.

The problem might *seem* to be that the band is travelling *too fast* to measure it with a ruler. But the problem is really not that it is travelling so fast that we can't *quite* get the ruler to it, as if we were trying to catch someone up in a relay race, but unable to do so because she is running a little too fast. The problem is that the band is moving at all, at any speed. If we are standing still, we will never catch the runner ahead if she is running at any speed at all.

Wittgenstein was able to put his finger on the false and misleading picture which stands behind the different puzzles about time. The picture is Figure 2, the picture of a time as a moving band. The consequence of the picture is that we think that the concept of measure has the same kind of application both in the case of a moving band and in the case of a passing time.

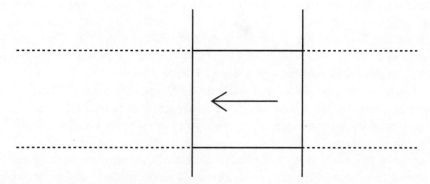

Figure 2   Wittgenstein's Travelling Band

Readers of Wittgenstein sometimes complain that he does not really *solve* the puzzles about time. There is some truth to this. But what he does do is to remove the false picture which distorts the logic of the initial propositions. This process leaves the way clear *not to misunderstand* the initial propositions, and this is what Wittgenstein understood by the *dissolution* of a philosophical problem. 'Philosophy,' he says, 'as we use the word, is a fight against the fascination which forms of expression exert upon us.'[12] We use the apparently similar expressions 'measuring time' and 'measuring distance'. The apparently similar grammar of these expressions conceals enormous logical differences, including the one which comes to a head in Aristotle's Rule and in the puzzle of the properties of the past.

How we can we measure time, for example, when time will not stay still to be measured, and apparently evades the application of Aristotle's Rule? This is the puzzle of the impossibility of measuring time given earlier. How do we measure time? When the false picture of the travelling band is removed, the question is surprisingly easy to answer.

Let us measure the time it takes to walk across the room. What do we do?

The first thing is to have a watch. There are two important conditions which must be satisfied by a watch if it is to allow us to measure a time.

1   The hands must move at a regular and unchanging rate.

2   There must be fixed and equal units marked off, through which the hands move.

The standard units are of course seconds, minutes and hours.

Second, we must coordinate the beginning of the walking to be measured with a point on the face of the clock. So we say, 'Let's start the walk when the second hand is at the 12.' And we do it (see Figure 3). We start the walk, with heels against one wall of the room, and then, as the walk finishes, when our toecaps hit the far wall, we look again at the watch to see where the second hand is now. It is just passing the four-second mark. So we say, 'It took four seconds to walk across the room', or 'The time it takes to cross the room is four seconds.' We have measured time! And it was not very difficult! How has the trick been done?

Or have we merely measured *a* time? Suppose we have. Then what would it be to measure time itself? People might just as well say, when you measure my foot for a new shoe, that you haven't measured space *itself*, but only *a* space. Or they might say that you haven't measured a space, but only my foot. But then what on earth *is* measuring 'space itself'? Sitting in a cosmic expanse and waving a ruler around? What, for that matter, is 'space itself'? Is it the *whole* of space?

Figure 3   Measuring Time

C
The Initial Propositions

Since we can measure time, it seems that there must be something wrong with Aristotle's Rule, which seems to imply that we can't. What is it? Consider the following proposition.

> The present century has been one of war and turmoil, like all past centuries.

There are several important things to notice about the way the concept of *the present* works in examples like this.

1   The word 'present', which is here an adjective, is what has been called 'substantive-hungry'. It is hungry for a noun. The phrase 'the present', in this usage, must be completed by a word, like 'century' or 'decade'. The completing word does not have to be the name of a stretch of time, though. We use the word in connection with the present *crisis*, the present *holder of the office*, and so on, meaning the crisis which is happening *now*, or the person who holds the office *now*.

2   Exactly the same word (the 'present') can apply in exactly the same sense to larger or smaller stretches of time, provided that a different noun completes the adjective. This is the retrenchability argument in reverse gear. We can speak of the present century, but also the present decade, the present year, the present month, the present week, the present day, the present hour, the present minute and the present second. There are no smaller divisions than seconds in common use.

3   'Present' in the sense in which it is used in the above proposition has,

very roughly, the sense of 'the one we are in'. In 1998 the 'present century' is: that stretch of a hundred years which *contains* or includes this year, 1998. On 30 June, the present month is: that month which contains or includes today, 30 June, namely June. At 11:30 p.m. the present hour is that hour which includes the present minutes, namely the twelfth hour.

So far from being vanishingly small, and having 'no length', as St Augustine says in the puzzle of the retrenchability of the present, the 'present' is indefinitely expansible, and can cover a period of *any* amount of time, provided only, presumably, that it doesn't cover all of time. The present century is no less present than the present second. There is some indication of the truth of this in the fact that there is a serious question as to *what* sense St Augustine's durationless instants are themselves present. The answer that they are the moments which we are in invites the further question of why the application of *this* concept is being denied to minutes and centuries.

This is the answer to the retrenchability puzzle. St Augustine asks whether a hundred years can be present. 'If', he says, 'it is the first year of the hundred, then that year is present, but the other ninety-nine are still in the future.' He concludes that, 'Thus a hundred years cannot be present.' When he says 'that year is present', what he must mean, according to point 1 above, is that 'that year is the present *year*.' This is true. But it does not have any tendency to undermine the truth that this *century* is the present *century*. The fact that not all the *years* of the present century are present does not show that the century is not present – that is, not the present *century* – in the sense given in point 3. The retrenchability puzzle ignores point 3, then.

It might seem as if there is a free-standing substantive use of 'the present' which simply means *the present*. But *what* does this mean? Does it mean 'the present time'? If so, time in what measure? Is the present time intended the present century, the present year, the present month, or what?

St Augustine cannot reply, to *this* argument, that what is meant by 'the present', without a qualification, is 'some point of time which cannot be divided into even the minutest parts of moments'. For the purpose of his use of the retrenchability argument is precisely to establish that this durationless instant is all the present can be.

What St Augustine is relying on in the analysis of the present is an application of Aristotle's Rule. This application says that in order for anything to be measured as present, it must all be present at once. What 'present' means here is *'entirely* present'. By this application of Aristotle's Rule, it cannot be truly said that I see the Atlantic Ocean from Cape Cod, because not *all* of the Atlantic Ocean is present at Cape Cod. However, this violates the truth of point 3. It confuses 'present' or 'in' with 'present in all its parts' or 'wholly in'. It has the consequence that the only place the Atlantic Ocean could be is in the whole of the Atlantic basin.

According to St Augustine, propositions about the present where the phrase 'the present' does not mean a durationless instant, but a longer stretch of time, are all false. For him:

> The present century has been one of war and turmoil, like all other centuries.

is false, because the century in question is never present. But his implicit analysis is absurd.

↓

This year is Y, and the hundred-year period, all of whose years are included in the year Y, has been one of war and turmoil, like all other hundred-year periods.

St Augustine is bound to think that the proposition that the century is present is false, because he thinks that it is equivalent to the above analysis, which contains the absurdity 'the hundred-year period, all of whose years are contained in the present year'. Instead of concluding that that proposition is false, and that a century cannot be truly present, he should have concluded that his analysis was false.

The true analysis is:

↓

This year is Y, and the hundred-year period which includes Y has been one of war and turmoil, like all other hundred-year periods.

Note that the analysis of 'the present century' includes the demonstrative 'this' in 'this year' essentially.

This analysis will help us to understand Aristotle's Rule, and what, it turns out, is St Augustine's misapplication of it. The application of the Rule says that in order to measure a time, all parts of the time must be present *at the same time*.

A year is a time, St Augustine thinks, but happening at the same time means happening at the same unextended instant. So what Aristotle's Rule requires, that a year should be present in one unextended instant, is impossible.

Or is it? For there is, *in the sense given in point 3*, a time at which even the whole year is present, and this time is, of course, the whole year! In order to measure a hundred-yard race lasting say ten seconds, the whole race must be run in *one* ten-second period. And this is exactly what happens when the race is measured in the normal way. It would be unmeasurable if it were continually broken up, say for a film, into different 'takes', with intervals of time in between. Then we *could* say that Aristotle's Rule was violated. In the ordinary case of measuring a time, however, it has not been violated.

What has gone wrong with St Augustine's application of the Rule is that he is working *both* with 3, the given or pre-analytical extensible sense of the present piece of time ('extensible' meaning that it can be extended ad lib from a second to an hour or a day or a week or a month or a year or a century), *and* with his own notion in which a time is an unextended moment. Then the problem of the year being present becomes the problem of cramming it into one unextended instant.

The solution to the puzzle about the non-existence of the present is that there can be changes in 'the present', provided the phrase is understood as in point 3. There can be changes in the present month; for example, a change of house or a change in the weather.

The puzzle of the properties of the past also falls into line. What does it mean to say, as St Augustine says, that the past is long?

> The past is long.

The difficulty here is that it is unclear what the proposition is actually intended to assert. Is St Augustine meaning 'the past' to refer to all times past since the creation? Does he mean that there is a lot of the past – more, indeed, every second? In this case, the proposition means that the period of time between the creation and now is long. This in turn means that there are many of whatever the chosen units of time are, say years, in this period.

↓

> This year is Y, and the number of years in the period from the creation to Y is large.

'The past' is not the name of some giant bin of non-existence, into which the present years and the events in them unfortunately keep on tumbling, but which are preserved, God knows how, in memory. It is simply a measured period, a period which is related to some other set of regular events, namely those happening now. St Augustine's tendency not to understand this, and to think of the past as an invisible place, is clearly shown in the way he chooses to formulate his questions. 'If the future and the past exist, I want to know where they are.'[13] Would he be satisfied with 'In China' as an answer? What does the spatial metaphor 'where they are' really mean as applied to past and future?

What the analysis shows is that 'the past' fits the same logical pattern as 'the present'. The phrase 'the past' is substantive-hungry too. The analysis shows that what it really means is 'the period composed of past *years* or past measured times'. The adjective 'past' becomes the definite description 'the number of years in the period from the creation to Y'. And when 'the past' functions adjectivally, there is no mystery about the existence of the past, any more than there is any mystery about the existence of the last, which is what the last race of the day is. Compare:

> The last race has been run.

with

> The past year has been fun.
> ↓
> This year is Y, and the year before Y has been fun.

One can almost hear St Augustine bemoaning the absence of 'the last', and asking, '*Where*, if the last (race) exists, does it exist?'

D
Time and the Nature of Change

There have been two opposed views which try to explain the nature of time. One of these views, like St Augustine's, takes very seriously the passage of time. The other regards the passage of time as a myth, or at very best a misleading metaphor.[14]

> Often, however, those who proclaim the anisotropy[[15]] of time are not motivated by scientific considerations but are gripped by a certain sort of metaphysical picture. They have in mind that time is more than a fixed sequence of events ordered by such relations as *later than* and *simultaneous with*, but that it also contains a peculiar property – being *now* – which moves gradually along the array in the direction from past to future.[16]

The philosopher J.M.E. McTaggart produced a celebrated proof (or a notorious one, depending on your point of view) to show that time is impossible.[17] His conception of time is, like St Augustine's, of the 'moving now' variety. That is, for him time is a *now* which moves along a series of moments from earlier ones to later ones, lighting up each successively with its presence. This persuasive picture, he believed, correctly construed the form of propositions about time, but the logic was a contradictory one. Here he was also in agreement with St Augustine, who declared that time's presence is its tendency to absent itself.[18]

McTaggart makes a distinction between two types of position in time. There is what he calls the A-series, which locates temporal positions in the *past, present* and *future*. Then there is what he calls the B-series, which locates temporal positions with respect to whether they are *earlier than* or *later than* one another.[19]

McTaggart's argument has the following structure.

	(1)	The B-series requires time.
	(2)	Time requires change.
	(3)	Change requires the A-series.
But	(4)	The A-series is contradictory.
Now	(5)	Hence time requires the A-series [by (2) and (3), by a hypothetical syllogism, and reading ' – requires – ' as 'If – then – '].
And	(6)	The B-series requires the A-series [by (1) and (5), same reasoning].
So	(7)	A. Time does not exist [by (5) and (4), *modus tollens*].
	and	B. The A-series does not exist [from (4)].
	and	C. The B-series does not exist [by (6) and (4), *modus tollens*].

The heart of the argument is (4). McTaggart thought that time is contradictory or impossible because each event is both past, present and future, and that these are contradictory descriptions, in the sense that if something is past, it is not present, and if it is present it is not future, and so on. 'Past, present and future are incompatible determinations. Every event must be one or the other, but no event can be more than one.'[20]

McTaggart's problem here is ultimately Platonic. The flow of time prevents events from remaining unalterably what they are. Therefore they are not real *or the flow of time is not real*. Events are unquestionably real. So time is not real and it does not exist. McTaggart concluded that reality is a kind of eternity, which he called the C-series, defined by him as the A-series without time. 'There is a series – a series of the permanent relations to one another of those realities which in time are events . . . [which] is not temporal, for it involves no change, but only an order.'[21] This analysis and proof of eternity is part of the interest of McTaggart's argument.

Let us look at step (3).[22] I believe it is mistaken, and that this is why McTaggart's celebrated conclusion for eternity does not follow. This does not of course prevent other steps in the argument from being invalid as well.

McTaggart thinks that the following analysis is correct. Let there be a hot poker which is taken from the fire at tea-time (t_1), and then, by t_2, becomes cold.

The poker changed from hot at t_1 to cold at t_2.
↓
The event of the poker being hot is present and the event of the poker being cold is future, and the event of the poker being cold is present and the event of the poker being hot is past.

Note that this is an analysis of 'changed', which disappears from the analysed proposition.

However, McTaggart also thinks that this analysis is contradictory. For it says of the poker being hot that it is *present*, and that it is *past*, and of the poker being cold that it is *future* and that it is *present*. How can anything which makes these contradictions possible itself be possible or exist?

One possibility which McTaggart rejected was a wholly B-series analysis of time, which ignores the distinctions between past, present and future, regarding these as merely relative to our own temporal 'position', just as the distinctions between far away and near are relative to our own temporal position. The formulation of such a B-series analysis is as follows.

The poker changed from hot at t_1 to cold at t_2.
↓
The poker is hot at t_1 and is cold at t_2, and t_1 is earlier than t_2.

On this view change or becoming is the presence of the *same* individual, the poker, at *different* times (t_1 and t_2), with *different* properties predicated of it (hot and cold) at these times. (Motion in this analysis would be a kind of change, the presence of the same individual at different times with different properties – (being in such-and-such a place) – predicated of it. Alternatively, change could be a kind of motion, the motion of an individual through a 'predicate space'.)

So the array of events in a B-series *does* have the resources to describe change, as in this two-event B-series matrix.

$$t_n \quad t_m$$
$$Ax \quad Bx$$

When A = H (H for 'hot') and x = p (p for 'poker') and n = 1, then 'Ax' is the event of the poker being hot at t_1, and when A = H ('H' for 'hot') and x = p (for 'poker', again) and B = C (C for 'cold') and m = 2, then 'Bx' is the event of the poker being cold at t_2. The partisans of the A-series will say that Hp and Cp are stuck timelessly in the aspic of the eternally unchanging matrix, and that the matrix does not include and cannot include real change – and all because it is a static *diagram*!

But there is in fact change represented in the matrix. The three conditions given in the analysis of the poker's change allow a description of change, just when x = x (naturally!) and A is not = B, and n < m.

Why did McTaggart wish to reject this commonsensical approach to change? His argument is that in changes described purely in B-series terms the earlier events so described would have to *cease to exist* in order to make way for the later ones. The event of the poker being hot, at t_1, would have to *cease* to exist in order to make way for the event of the poker being cold, at t_2. But this cannot happen, because 'An event can never cease to be an event.'[23] What McTaggart seems to be relying on is the idea that an event is essentially a happening, and a happening cannot not happen. The poker being cold is then a timelessly occurrent event.[24]

The main mistake, here, it seems to me, is to picture events as the basic elements in time and change, and to conceive them as bead-like things strung along the positions in the series of times. Then the only kind of change there can be is, as McTaggart puts it, a change which 'yet leave[s] the event the same event'.[25] That is, the only kind of change can be an A-series change, which does not touch the event but does touch its relative position in the sliding by of future, present and past. But it is not events which change, it is things which change, and the event *is* the change. Here, funnily enough, McTaggart is not wrong. The change does not itself change. That is, the event is *the poker cooling*; this is to be understood as the poker losing heat. If our world is restricted to events, conceived as McTaggart conceives them, then indeed there are no resources within the B-series for change, and there can be no changes save A-series changes. But there is more to change than the popping-up of a subject pre-packaged, with a predicate, as an event. Time and change are so to speak *within* the event, as the analysed proposition makes clear, and what moves or changes is not time itself, but the object, from one state to another.

The measurement of time is the coordination of movements and changes, such as walking across the room, with changes in a regular and quantized parallel set of movements, of the hands of a clock or watch, or of the sun in the sky. Aristotle went so far as to identify this measure with time itself, in his dictum that 'Time is a measure of motion.'[26]

Whatever the ultimate merit of McTaggart's arguments for rejecting a B-series account of change, they sharpen our understanding of what time is and, more importantly perhaps, is *not* like, and how it can be so unlike most of the things within our common experience. These arguments also prepare the way to understand persistence through time and change, particularly of persons.

Historical Note

The stranger and more interesting features of time have been highlighted by metaphysical A-series views of time, which regard it as a physically real moving *now*, or which represent it as like a force or a dimension. B-series views, descending from Aristotle, have taken it as a secondary feature of a matrix of events. In the seventeenth century Newton defined 'absolute, true and mathematical time' or 'duration' as something which 'of itself, and from its own nature, flows equably without relation to anything external',[27] an A-series view, and distinguished it from 'relative, apparent and common time', which is 'some sensible and external (whether accurate and unequable) measure of duration by means of motion'. In the same century Leibniz argued that space and time are 'purely relative', and that just as space 'is an order of co-existences', so 'time is an order of succes-sions'.[28] In the twentieth century, apart from metaphysical views like McTaggart's, logic and physics have tended to converge on a B-series view.

Notes

1 Aristotle, from Book IV of the *Physics*, trans. R.P. Hardie and R.K. Gaye, in *The Basic Works of Aristotle*, ed. Richard McKeon, New York, Random House, 1941, p. 289, 217b30–218a5.
2 St Augustine, *Confessions*, trans. F.J. Sheed, New York, Sheed and Ward, 1943, p. 271.
3 Ibid., pp. 272–273.
4 Ibid., p. 276.
5 Ibid., p. 283.
6 Ibid., p. 284.
7 Ludwig Wittgenstein, *The Blue and Brown Books*, Oxford, Blackwell, 1958, p. 26.
8 Ibid.
9 Ibid., p. 27.
10 'If a divisible thing is to exist, it is necessary that, when it exists, all or some of its parts

must exist. But of time some parts have been, while others are going to be, and no part of it *is*, though it is divisible.' Aristotle, *Physics*, Book IV, p. 289, 218a5.

11 Wittgenstein, *Blue and Brown Books*, p. 26.

12 Ibid., p. 27.

13 St Augustine, *Confessions*, p. 274.

14 See for example D.C. Williams, 'The Myth of Passage', *Journal of Philosophy* XLVIII, No. 15 (1951), pp. 457–472, also in Jonathan Westphal and Carl Levenson, eds, *Time*, Indianapolis/Cambridge, Mass., Hackett, 1993, p. 131. The two key questions Williams puts to those who believe in the passage of time are: (1) If time moves, what does time move *through*? If it moves through time of any sort, then there is a form of time which does *not* move. (2) If time moves, we must be able to attach sense to the question of at what speed it moves. But speed is defined as distance covered over time. Hence the speed of time is the distance it travels in a given time. What does 'distance' mean here? If it is temporal distance, then the speed of time is the time it travels in a given time, which is absurd.

15 'Anisotropy' is a significant lack of symmetry between the two directions of the temporal continuum; 'isotropy' means that a continuum is essentially the same in all directions. Space seems to be isotropic.

16 Paul Horwich, *Asymmetries in Time*, Cambridge, Mass., MIT Press, 1987, pp. 15–16.

17 J.M.E. McTaggart, 'The Unreality of Time', *Mind* xviii (1908), pp. 457–474.

18 'Thus we can affirm that time *is* only in that it tends towards not-being.' St Augustine, *Confessions*, p. 271.

19 McTaggart, 'Unreality of Time', p. 458.

20 Ibid., p. 468.

21 Ibid., p. 461.

22 For interesting discussion of the challenges that can be made to the other steps in McTaggart's argument, see Horwich, *Asymmetries in Time*, Ch. 2.

23 McTaggart, 'Unreality of Time', p. 459.

24 I criticized the very idea of the *existence*, as opposed to the occurrence, of an event in 'Sources of Error in the Metaphysics of Time', *Philosophical Investigations* 19, No. 2 (1996), pp. 131–139.

25 McTaggart, 'Unreality of Time', p. 460.

26 Aristotle, *Physics*, in McKeon, 1941, p. 294.

27 Isaac Newton, *Principia*, Scholium to the Definitions, I, trans. Andrew Motte, ed. Florian Cajori, Berkeley, Calif., University of California Press, 1947, p. 6.

28 'The Leibniz–Clarke Correspondence', Leibniz's Third Paper, in 'Correspondence with Clarke', in *Leibniz: Philosophical Writings*, ed. G.H. Parkinson, London, Dent, 1973, p. 211.

Reading

J.R. Lucas, *A Treatise on Space and Time*, London, Methuen, 1973.

G.E.L. Owen, 'Aristotle on Time', in *Logic, Science and Dialectic: Collected Papers*, ed. Martha Nussbaum, Ithaca, N.Y., Cornell University Press, 1986.

*J.J.C. Smart, 'Time', in *Encyclopedia of Philosophy*, Vol. 8, ed. Paul Edwards, New York, Macmillan, 1967.

*Jonathan Westphal and Carl Levenson, eds, *Time*, Indianapolis, Ind./Cambridge, Mass., Hackett, 1993.

7
Personal Identity
What Am I?

A
The Problem

The problem of personal identity can be formulated easily enough. Consider the various different physical and personality characteristics which a single person has in different periods of life.

The Puzzle of Personal Identity Through Change
At birth, there is a small organism without much intellectual life and without a highly differentiated personality. In childhood there is a larger little person, with a definite character and interests. In adolescence, a creature takes its place, sometimes different enough to be thought by its parents to belong to a completely different species. In middle age, there is a rather different-looking person, with differently coloured hair, a different weight and a different psychology. In old age, there is a person of a possibly completely different character, with a memory of childhood events which may be clearer than the memory of the middle-aged person. With these differences there is no single group of personal and physical characteristics which counts as that of *the* characteristics of the person. There is nothing which endures the same and is present at all the different stages of life.

There is an extreme and mistaken form of the problem which goes as follows.

(1) X (age 3) is 3 ft tall, blond, and lives at Broadstone Cottage in Forest Row, Sussex.
(2) Mr Y (age 47) is 6 ft 2 in tall, white-haired, and lives on Valley Vista Road in Pocatello, Idaho.
(3) X is not Mr Y.[1]
(4) X is Jonathan Westphal.
(5) Mr Y is Jonathan Westphal.
(6) Jonathan Westphal is not Jonathan Westphal.

Something has evidently gone badly wrong. (6) must be false, even if there is no such thing as something called identity, because (6) is a contradiction. But (4) and (5) seem to be true, as do (1) and (2). And Leibniz's Law is obviously true.

The problem lies not with the content of the propositions in the argument, but with confusions about truth and time in the use of the past and present tenses in which propositions (1) and (2) are stated. For it is true of X, the small blond boy, that he *is* tall and white-haired, and lives on Valley Vista Road, Pocatello, Idaho. And it is true of Mr Y that he *lived* at Broadstone Cottage and was 3 ft tall and blond in 1954. So there is nothing true of X which is not also true of Y, and Leibniz's Law is preserved.

The difficulty can be easily fixed. We need to make sure that the argument is not being made both in 1954, in which case the tense of proposition (2) is wrong, and in 1998, in which case the tense of proposition (1) is wrong, by flagging the time at which what the proposition states is claimed to be true. With this device, (1) would become (1'): X (age 3) *was* 3 ft tall and blond *in 1954*, and in *1954 lived* at Broadstone Cottage in Forest Row, Sussex. We need to fix a time at which the argument is being made, because its verbs are tensed.

Another way of achieving the same end would be to use a timeless present tense in which it could be stated, without commitment to the year, that X is *blond-in-1954* and Y is *grey-in-1998*. There is then no contradiction in saying that both predicates 'grey-in-1998' and 'blond-in-1954' are true of Y, at any time.

Reverting now to the substantial problem, one familiar and interesting though controversial answer to the puzzle of personal identity through change is that it is the soul which provides identity over time. What makes it the case that the small baby and the fully grown man can be said to be the same person is that they have the same soul.

X is the same person as Y.
↓
X has the same soul as Y.

Yet what makes it the case that X, standing before me in the identity parade, is the same person as Y, the man whom I saw running out of the bank on the day of the robbery? Not, surely, that they have the same soul. It is *true* that they have the same soul, if X is Y, but this is not what his sameness with Y consists of, any more than having the same thumb is what his sameness consists of, just because it is true.

There is also the difficulty that the soul of X, if it changes over time in any way, must be factored into the problem of personal identity through change. X's soul will then be one of many characteristics which form part of the problem, not the solution.

The picture at work here is of a changing Platonic underworld, consisting of the different stages of a person's life, and hovering about them a single, unchanging and perfect entity, the soul of the person, which is the source of unity and identity. The picture of identity is of something which is *given* to X, a characteristic like eye-colour, which is *given* by the genes of the parents. X has blue eyes, and X has identity or an identity. If we remember that X 'having identity' is 'same person as' being true of X and someone else, then we will be less tempted to think of identity as a characteristic of X, still less of it as a characteristic common to X and Y.

It should also be noted that *problems* of identity arise when there is doubt or uncertainty about identity. This seems obvious, but it is the beginning of wisdom in these matters to see that what a proposition asserting identity does is to *remove* doubt or undesirable ignorance. Questions about inheritances, passport documents, paternity suits, guilt or innocence in criminal proceedings: these are the questions outside philosophy to which propositions about personal identity are the answer.

Consider a case parallel to the personal identity case. What makes the car Z1 which I owned twenty years ago the same car as the one I found in my brother's barn this summer, Z2? Z1 was almost new, ding- and dent-free, in good running order. Z2 is rusted and won't start, and has a bright orange door. Let us say Z1 and Z2 are the same car.

Z1 is the same car as Z2.
↓
Z1 has the same soul as Z2.

Cars don't have souls, however. It follows that Z1 does not have the same soul as Z2, because it doesn't have a soul at all. So by *modus tollens* Z1 and Z2 are not the same car. But this is absurd. So it must be the analysis which is false.

One might try saying that in the case of cars the soul of the car is the principle of identity, that is, the thing in virtue of which we are entitled to say that they are the same car. Then the final analysis would be, 'Z1 and Z2 have the principle in virtue of which Z1 and Z2 are the same car.' This will not do as an analysis, though, because it does not advance beyond the proposition to be analysed. We go from 'Z1 and Z2 are the same car' to 'Z1 and Z2 have the principle in virtue of which Z1 and Z2 are the same car.' The whole point of the analysis was to identify this principle, and this has not been done.

In the practical problems of the identification and reidentification of cars, for title purposes or those of sale or insurance, no matter what the differences between Z1 and Z2 may be, if they share the same VIN or vehicle identification number, they are counted as the same car. The VIN is stamped into the chassis or frame. (The analogue for this in the case of persons would presumably be the skeleton. This is not, however, a plausible candidate for identity in the case of persons, as orthopaedic surgery is too far advanced to prevent one from contemplating the possibility of a completely plastic skeleton.) The VIN carries the essential information about the identity of the car, and this suggests a possibility for the case of the person.

X is the same person as Y.
↓
The DNA of X is the same DNA as the DNA of Y.

This analysis provides a now commonly accepted test of identity in cases of assault, rape and murder, and in those involving paternity. It has achieved the same definitive status in the courts as the fingerprint test, except with a much wider possible application, as it does not depend on the suspect having left large, greasy fingerprints about. As a test it is useful for four reasons.

1 It works with a tissue sample from any part of the body.

2 It works with very small amounts of tissue.

3 A DNA profile is unique, like a fingerprint.

4 DNA is very stable, in the sense that a person's DNA profile will not change.

However, though the DNA proposition gives a good[2] *test* of identity, it is not adequate to provide an *analysis* of identity. This is an important distinction. Testing the performance of a metal, for example, is a very different thing from analysing its substance. Though the DNA test can tell us *when* X and Y are identical, it cannot tell us *what* that identity is or of what it consists.

Furthermore, DNA can itself change through mutation, say one caused by radiation. Does this mean, given the DNA analysis of identity, that the person X before the mutation is not the same person as Y, the person after the mutation? Plainly not, especially if the change in the DNA is a slight one.

This raises the question of *DNA identity*. What changes are to be regarded as sufficiently slight to allow us to say that sample s contains the same DNA as sample r, which is overall the same, but with slight differences due to exposure to radiation? What is the analysis of the following proposition?

> The DNA in sample n is the same DNA as the DNA in sample m.

Consider the following so-called 'point mutations', single nucleotide changes in a DNA molecule. Such mutations can be completely neutral, in the sense that they have no phenotypic effect. The normal sample is n, the mutated ones m and m'.[3]

> Sample n: normal
> . . . CTG TCA CCT GTA CCA CCT. . .
> . . . GAC AGT GGA CAT GGT GGA. . .
> Sample m: 'substitution'
> . . . CTG **G**CA CCT GTA CCA CCT . . .
> . . . GAC **C**GT GGA CAT GGT GGA . . .

Or consider m with **G** 'deleted', resulting in:

> Sample m': 'deletion'
> . . . CTG CAC CTG TAC CAC CT . . .
> . . . GAC GTG GAC ATG GTG GA . . .

We need an account of identity in order to analyse the proposition about the sameness of DNA samples and to decide whether mutation is consistent with identity, and if so how much so. When are n and m sufficiently dissimilar not to count as samples of the same DNA? How much variation will DNA tolerate? What in the philosophical sense is the *substance* of a DNA sample? An analysis of identity in general and of persons in particular is just what is being sought, with the aid of the DNA-based philosophical analysis. In other words the DNA analysis does not give an analysis of identity, but presupposes it. This is also true of the other competing analyses of personal identity of particular objects and substances. In the words of Anthony Quinton:

> No general account of the identity of a kind of individual thing
> can be given which finds that identity in the presence of another

individual thing within it. For the question immediately arises, how is the identity through time of the identifier to be established? It, like the thing it is supposed to identify, can present itself at any one time only as it is at that time. However alike its temporally separate phases may be, they still require to be identified as parts of the same, continuing thing.[4]

B
The Prince and the Cobbler and the Two Criteria

In a famous passage in the *Essay Concerning Human Understanding* John Locke raised the first of what came to be called 'puzzle cases' about personal identity.[5] A puzzle case is a thought-experiment or imagined or imaginary case designed to test our principles about what constitutes personal identity. Locke is aiming to show that 'the soul alone, in [a] change of bodies, would scarce to any one, but to him that makes the soul the man, be enough to make the same man.' He asks us to imagine that the soul of a prince is transported into the body of a cobbler. His conclusion is that the body makes the man, while the person is made by consciousness, and so he makes a distinction between the man and the person. The person is determined by consciousness or memory.

> For should the soul of a prince, carrying with it the consciousness of the prince's past life, enter and inform the body of a cobbler as soon as deserted by his own soul, every one sees he would be the same person with the prince, accountable only for the prince's actions: but who would say it was the same man? The body too goes to making the man, and would, I guess, to everybody determine the man in this case; wherein the soul, with all its princely thoughts about it, would not make another man.[6]

Let us complicate Locke's case a little, in such a way as also to redress the balance against the cobbler, whose soul, in Locke's description of the puzzle case, merely 'deserts' his body, presumably to make way for the prince. Let us imagine that the soul of the cobbler, carrying with it his consciousness, also enters the body of the prince. Leaving the soul out of the problem, for the reasons given above in the objections to the analysis of personal identity as soul, and taking the soul merely as the seat of consciousness, this gives the following picture.

	A Prince		B Cobbler
Consciousness	C_P	$\leftrightarrow$	C_C
Body	B_P		B_C

Locke is beginning with the conception of the prince as having both a consciousness and a body. In this situation, A is both the man the prince, because A has $<B_P>$, and the person the prince, because it has $<C_P>$. After the transfer of consciousness, we arrive at the following situation.

A	B
C_C	C_P
B_P	B_C

In this situation, according to Locke, A is the person the cobbler, in the sense that the answer to the question, 'Which person is A?' is 'The cobbler', and the man the prince, in the sense that the answer to the question 'Which man is A?' is 'The prince'. B is the prince, considered as a person, and the cobbler, considered as a man 'to every one besides himself', in Locke's words.

One important preliminary issue can be quickly settled. It is sometimes said that $<C_P + B_C>$ must be taken to be the cobbler, having an attack of powerful delusional fantasy, and imagining that he is a prince, or it is said that at least this cannot be immediately ruled out as an explanation and analysis. $<C_P + B_C>$ is the cobbler, on this view, but the cobbler is suffering from some form of mental illness. Yet this response will not do if the apparent memories of $<C_P + B_C>$ are specific and accurate enough to count as bona fide memory. For in that case the memory experiences are not delusional fantasies, if that is taken to mean that they are not true. Suppose, for example, that $<C_P + B_C>$ when asked can describe in which drawer in which chest of drawers the prince keeps his real tennis socks. Suppose also that the only person with this information is the prince. Suppose also that $<C_C + B_P>$ is unable to 'remember' where he keeps 'his' socks. Suppose finally that the prince has always been and is known to have been excessively attentive to his dress on court, as well as in court, and keeps very careful track of his tennis accessories and equipment. Then the case seems overwhelmingly strong for saying either that $<C_P + B_C>$ is the prince, or that $<C_P + B_C>$ is not the prince, but is clairvoyant. Suppose clairvoyance, at least for the whereabouts of socks, does not exist. Then $<C_P + B_C>$ is the prince, and consciousness determines the identity of persons. Then:

X is the same person as Y.
↓
X's consciousness is the same consciousness as Y's.

This analysis is open to a devastating objection, however. In order to state this objection, it must be more precisely formulated as:

↓
X's consciousness contains a memory of Y's consciousness.

For example, Sir Winston Churchill's consciousness in 1964 contained memories of Winston Churchill delivering a famous wartime fighting speech in 1940. Or, better expressed, without the ponderous and obscure reference to consciousness, in 1964 Sir Winston remembered delivering the famous fighting wartime speech in 1940. Accordingly by the memory criterion the elderly person living in Kent known as Sir Winston Churchill was the same person as the prime minister of 1940. Yet Sir Winston in 1964 had no memories of the prime minister in 1940 *when the latter was asleep*! This tells us that the memory criterion makes Sir Winston in 1964 not to have been the same person as the prime minister snoozing in No. 10 Downing Street, London, on such-and-such a hectic day in 1940. This is of course false. Sir Winston, c. 1964, is indeed the person who was snoozing in No. 10 Downing Street, London, on such-and-such a day in 1940 and who subsequently gave the speech.

One thing that needs fixing right away is 'contains'. It must be replaced by 'contains *or could contain*'. For mere forgetfulness does not seem sufficient to make a different person, and even amnesia does not. It seems that what is important is the *possibility* of remembering, as opposed to the actuality.

There have been several further suggested emendations to Locke's analysis. One of the most important of these is 'psychological connectedness'.[7] Here the requirement is only that the links of memory between X and Y be *indirect*. On this view, the mistake of the memory analysis or criterion is the mistake that would be made by someone who insisted that in order to be called the same bridge, end x, in Manhattan, and end y, in Queens, would have to be touching, which is absurd because it eliminates the span between them. The correct analysis on this view – or a more correct analysis – requires merely that X and Y are indirectly connected in the sense that X can remember what went on the day before, and the day before X can remember much of what went on the day before that, and so on, even though X cannot directly remember a thing about her Y-state.

This emendation gets around a celebrated objection made by the Scottish philosopher Thomas Reid. The objection is that one can imagine a case in which there is a general who remembers having been a brave captain, but cannot remember having been a schoolboy. Add to this also that the captain can remember having been the schoolboy. Given that memory generates identity, from the memory criterion:

> it follows, if there be any truth in logic, that the general is the same person with him who was flogged at school. But the general's consciousness does not reach so far back as his flogging: therefore, according to Mr. Locke's doctrine, he is not the same person who was flogged. Therefore the general is, and at the same time is not, the same person with him who was flogged at school.[8]

↓

Z's consciousness could contain a memory of Y's consciousness, and A's consciousness could contain a memory of Z's consciousness, and B's consciousness could contain a memory of A's consciousness, and X's consciousness could contain a memory of B's consciousness.

Instead of one big memory arch between X and Y,

X   Y

there are many little arches:

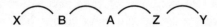

X   B   A   Z   Y

Now it does not matter that X cannot directly remember Y, because X could remember some B-state, of which it is true that B could remember some A-state, and so on to Y. This takes care of the sleep-gap objection, by 'island hopping' the states of unconsciousness during the nights, and also of gaps created by amnesia for much earlier states at any point in the sequence of arches. All that is required is that some member of the sequence should or could remember *something* of what went on the previous day, some experience of a state which contains a memory of some experience which . . . contains a memory of Y.

Yet what if all that X can remember is Y and nothing in between? This is what Perry calls 'the Senile General Case', by contrast with Reid's Brave Officer Case.[9] It is the case connectedness analysis was supposed to *avoid*. Yet it must be possible that the single arch X to Y is all that a senile general can remember, having forgotten all the intervening years. The Lockean analysis in terms of memory is unable to accommodate simultaneously cases in which what is missing are the middle arches B–A–Z, and cases in which what is missing is the central arch X–Y, since one excludes the other. This has to do with the random and discontinuous nature of memory of different Xs, Bs, As, Zs and Ys. Identity requires by contrast a completely non-random and continuous connection.

Furthermore, the memory criterion does not reach far enough, even in the amended version. For it does not reach back to birth. Presumably we do want to say that such-and-such a person was *born* so many years ago, even if there is the road-block of so-called childhood amnesia.

Locke is arguing for an analysis or criterion of personal identity which is non-bodily: consciousness (of previous states) or *memory*. The difficulty with the *memory criterion* or analysis is that it lacks the right kind of continuity, the kind possessed by the person, and seemingly provided by his or her body, at least for practical legal and other identification purposes. A second criterion which has been suggested is the so-called *body criterion* or analysis.

X is the same person as Y.
↓
X has the same body as Y.

What are we to make of cases, though, like Locke's of the prince and the cobbler, which today, perhaps, might be diagnosed as cases of multiple personality, at least, in Locke's original description, for the cobbler. What would make this diagnosis utterly convincing, but which is itself completely improbable, is the kind of accuracy of memory which the prince's consciousness, in whatever body, would have about his own affairs.

Suppose that multiple personality is a fact. Then, assuming the equivalence of person and personality, the body criterion is wrong, and presupposes too much in the way of empirical findings in psychology. It is worth noting that the concept of multiple personality has seemed to presuppose a Lockean or dualist or anti-physical analysis of identity, meaning by 'dualist' here a theory in which mind or person and body are distinct entities. But 'such concepts [as reincarnation and possession of the body by evil spirits or devils] have gradually been abandoned in favor of other explanations', including hysterical associative reaction and temporal lobe abnormalities.[10]

Furthermore, it seems that, like DNA and like consciousness, considered as an entity, the body criterion falls foul of Quinton's methodological principle that 'No general account of the identity of a kind of individual thing can be given which finds that identity in the presence of another individual thing within it.' Here the first individual thing is the person, taken to be the complex of consciousness and body, <C + B>, and the second individual thing is the body, <B>. On the other hand, perhaps Quinton's principle is a little too stringent. It is true that making the body the criterion of personal identity raises the question of what bodily identity is, yet it does reduce the problem of personal identity in particular to the problem of the general identity of organisms and physical objects. This would be progress, if the general problem had a solution. Let us turn to a case of the identity of a physical object which is not a person, but a ship. Ships and boats are often treated as persons or rather as having personalities.

C
The Ship of Theseus

'The Ship of Theseus' is the description of a problem of object identity which has apparently alarming consequences for the concept of personal identity.

> The First Replacement Puzzle
> Theseus has a wooden ship, the Ship of Theseus, which he keeps in good repair. A repair involves replacing an unsound board or beam with a new one. Over the years Theseus replaces every single piece of the ship. This raises the question whether the ship at the end can be called *the same ship* as the ship he started with. Suppose the original ship is covered by marine insurance, and suppose that the 'new' ship, with the new boards and beams, burns down at sea. Is it covered by the original policy or not?

If the answer to this seems a simple affirmative, consider another possibility.

> The Second Replacement Puzzle
> Theseus keeps the old beams and boards in a barn, perhaps for firewood, but after a time realizes that he has been over-zealous in his repairs, sands the lumber and treats it with preservative oils, and reconstructs the old ship. Which ship is covered by the original marine insurance, the one in the barn or the one which burned down at sea?

In Figure 4, Theseus takes delivery of the original ship S_1 at t_1. At t_2 he begins repairs. The dotted line represents the growing pile of lumber in the barn. By t_3 none of the original parts remains in S_7. S_5 is reconstructed from the lumber at t_4. At t_5, the new 'old' ship S_6 is launched, and at t_6 the ship made of newer materials, S_{10}, burns down and sinks (it could be called the S_{10} Blazer).

The question for the insurance adjuster is whether S_{10} or S_{11} is S_1. (Or anyway this is *a* question.) The application of the case of the Ship of Theseus to personal identity is obvious. The matter of the physical parts of persons is continuously being replaced, according to rumours, so that none of the matter in our bodies at any one time is older than seven years. Has anybody checked? What if the matter which passes out of my body were kept, and the original person-minus-seven-years were reconstructed? Which would deserve to be called by my name, the present person or the 'reconstructed' one?

We need to ask the question *why* such a case and that of the Ship of Theseus are so puzzling. The answer I propose to give is that in it two kinds of principle of identity come into conflict and are perfectly balanced.

The first kind of principle is one of continuity. If X is identical with Y, then, by this principle, there is a continuity between X and Y. Thus if Y is the person who was born in Forest Row, Sussex, in Broadstone Cottage, on

t_1 Delivery of S_1.

t_2 First repairs on S_1.

t_3 No original planks remain from S_1.

t_4 Reconstruction of S_1.

t_5 Launching of S_6.

t_6 Sinking of S_{10}.

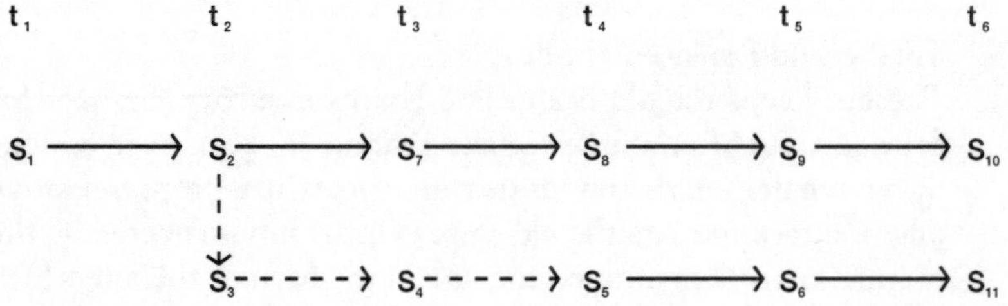

Figure 4   The Ship of Theseus

14 January 1951, and a continuous path in space and time could be traced between the infant which was delivered then, and a person X in 1998, then Y is X. The question is whether *following* Y would lead one to X's door. One can even imagine a companion who follows Y around from 1951 to 1998 to make sure the continuity is not broken.

The second kind of principle is one of similarity. If X is identical with Y, then there must be some major similarities between X and Y. In the case of human persons, these could include history, basic personality and DNA. In the case of the Ship of Theseus, we would immediately reject a claim for the identity of X and Y, where X was a small, 4.2 metre dinghy and Y was a ship of the same size as the *QE2*. The two craft are not similar enough to be identical.

In the case of the Ship of Theseus, the principle of continuity would suggest that S_{10} is identical with S_1. The principle of similarity, however, would suggest that S_9 is. S_{10} might, for example, be made of a different kind of cheaper wood than S_9. At any rate, S_9 is a better candidate for identity with S_2 than S_{10} is, because S_{10} is *new*, and S_9 is not. In that case, though, S_{10} has a better claim to be S_1 and S_9 to be S_2. But S_1 and S_2 are certainly identical if anything is. Hence the perfect balance between the two principles.

This is I believe indirect evidence that the two principles jointly determine identity. For there must be some explanation of why cases like the Ship of Theseus are so puzzling and hard to decide. My answer is that it is a case in which the two joint principles of identity pull in opposite directions and return a different answer to the question of which ship is S_1.

D
A Resolution?

Identity in general, then, by the two principles extracted from the case of the Ship of Theseus, is continuity or what has been called numerical identity, plus similarity or what has been called qualitative identity. Why should this pair of principles not also define personal identity? Consider again the case of the prince and the cobbler. The difficulty, as far as the prince's wife is concerned, for the claim of the person now sleeping in her bed to *be* the cobbler, and to have a right to sleep with the cobbler's wife because he is married to her, is that the person now sleeping in her bed has a claim to physical continuity or numerical identity with the prince. The difficulty for the prince's lawyers, when someone who is apparently the cobbler claims the lands of the prince, is the lack of similarity or qualitative identity.

Yet psychologically $<B_C + C_P>$, the pretender, is or claims to be *numerically* identical with part of the prince, the 'mental' part, and psychologically the would-be adulterer, $<C_C + B_P>$ is or claims to be *numerically* identical with part of the cobbler, the 'mental' part. On the other hand, the pretender is *qualitatively* identical with the physical part of the cobbler, and the would-be adulterer is *qualitatively* identical with the physical part of the prince.

What has happened is that we are given, here as in the case of the Ship of Theseus, no further information about the cases beyond the mere fact of the transfer, and so we are left with two perfectly balanced principles, and no way of deciding their application. It is this further information which should decide these applications – what else could? All that we *are* given is a skeletal picture in which the crudity of the lines (two bodies swapping consciousnesses, like two women swapping husbands) absorbs and hypnotizes us and makes us forget that we do not fully understand what is being suggested.

Consider some difficult questions which cannot be answered without many more details about what the situation is the night after the transfer. These questions also bring out the ways in which the answers to the question of who is who are dependent on the further information.

Who is married to the princess? Who said the words (assuming that Locke's prince is an English-speaking Western Christian), 'I take you . . . to be my wife, to have and to hold from this day forward, for better for worse, for richer for poorer' and so on? Should the princess have a say in deciding this question? Her answer, it seems, could depend on a sense of *familiarity*, both physical and psychological, about the person in her bed. There is the question of his sense of familiarity as well. Some of his memories might be *body* memories, such as where to reach for his watch under the bed in the morning. Others might be undecidably bodily and mental, such as his sexual habits, and indeed his habits and preferences in general. Which complex $<B_C + C_P>$ or $<B_P + C_C>$ prefers champagne, and which prefers beer? Is this a physical or a psychological matter?

Suppose the prince committed a nasty murder the day before the transfer of his consciousness to the cobbler. (Perhaps this is *why* he mobilized the resources of the palace laboratory to arrange the transfer! In Locke's scenario it is not explained why or how the transfer takes place.) Who then is guilty and who should be hanged? In hanging $<B_C + C_P>$, the prince's consciousness, the authorities would no more be hanging the prince than if they hanged his horse. But then how *do* you hang a *consciousness*? And if intent is required for murder ('wrongful intentional killing of a person'), it will not do to hang $<B_C>$, in which there was no intent, nor yet $<B_P>$, from which the intent has fled with $<C_P>$.

Which complex should perform the tasks and duties of the cobbler? Which complex would be *better able* to perform these tasks? Without the memories of the cobbler, now implanted in the prince's body, the cobbler's body will not know where to find his tools. But without the easy familiarity with all sorts of actions and movements, some of it retained in muscle memory, the prince's body will be unable to cobble to a professional standard.

Which complex will speak with a working-class cobbler's accent, and which with the educated accents of the prince? This is important, because accent is not just a matter of consciousness, but also of the combined physical ability of the lips, palate, breath, tongue and teeth to form the correct sounds, and this is acquired only with physical practice. It is not a wholly mental ability. Can $<B_C + C_P>$ correctly pronounce the French word 'grenouille', for example? And if he cannot, does it matter that he has what might be classed as a delusional experience of having been taught to by a French governess?

Suppose that the cobbler is a woman. If after the transfer into her body of C_P he/she decides to join the army, and is rejected from a regiment which only accepts men, should she now sue the army for sexual discrimination (because she has the body of a woman) or should he now sue the army for an unfair employment practice, because he is a man, psychologically speaking, and has been wrongly rejected? But then which sex is a pure consciousness without a body? And does it make the slightest difference that that consciousness is for the moment in a body?

What happened on the night of the transfer? What does the prince remember? What does the cobbler remember?

The answers to such preliminary questions as these, it seems to me, will depend on the answers to a host of other empirical questions, which can and should be organized under the general principles of qualitative similarity and numerical continuity. If this is so, personal identity through change, like every other identity, is a matter of a sufficient similarity for us to judge the person changed but not completely changed. If the alteration is too great, for example if Y is a man and X is an elephant, then the matter decides itself empirically.

> X is the same person as Y.
> ↓
> There is physical and psychological continuity between X and Y, and X and Y are sufficiently similar.

This analysis does several things.

1 It insists on continuity, which is a commonsense requirement for identity.[11]
2 It limits the changes allowed for identity. In the analysis the question

of whether an identity exists between X and Y, that is, whether they are the same person, depends not on an underlying substance, but on empirical physical and psychological continuity and similarity. The analysis immediately rules out teletransportation. According to the analysis, when Captain Kirk is beamed aboard, he does not survive. What arrives on the *Enterprise* is merely a copy or a replica of the captain, no matter how like Captain Kirk, because it lacks continuity,[12] and the engineer who beams him aboard is open to a charge of murder.

3 It does not favour either the body or the mental criterion. What it favours is a net total of sameness over change, whether mental or physical.

Mach, the important nineteenth-century physicist and philosopher whose name is honoured in the Mach speed number, gave the same analysis in *The Analysis of Sensations*.[13]

> My friend may put on a different coat. His countenance may assume a serious or a cheerful expression. His complexion, under the effects of light or emotion, may change. His shape may be altered by motion, or be definitely changed. Yet the number of the permanent features presented, compared with the number of gradual alterations, is always so great, that the latter may be overlooked. It is the same friend with whom I take my daily walk ... Further, that complex of memories, moods and feelings, joined to a particular body (the human body), which is called the 'I' or 'Ego,' manifests itself as relatively permanent. I may be engaged on this or that subject, I may be quiet or cheerful, excited and ill-humored. Yet, pathological cases apart, enough durable features remain to identify the ego. Of course, the ego also is only of relative permanency.

All the same, the ego in Mach's sense may *as a matter of fact* be permanent. There is nothing in Mach's argument to show that there is not a set of memories, moods and feelings which, though they are not conscious, are yet accessible, either at death or even before. The panoramic recapitulation of life in near-death experiences is an example. As Mach's argument is empirical, the argument for a permanent psychological ego would be the same as for an impermanent ego in that it was as good or as bad as the evidence. For there is nothing in Mach's argument to show that a relatively permanent ego is a conceptual or logical impossibility, and that we might not 'wake up' or have further complexes of memories, moods and feelings after death, much as we wake up after a night's sleep, though without the set of experiences which we construct into our own body.

Assuming that the body does not survive death, the only thing that militates against survival after death on Mach's view is that the complex of memories, moods and feelings after death, if any, would have to have a very great similarity to the complex of memories, moods and feelings before death in order to offset the very great dissimilarity between the complex of memories, moods and feelings after death, minus the body, and the complex of memories, moods and feelings before death, with the body.

Historical
Note

Questions of personal identity arose historically in connection with dualism and questions about personal survival after death or immortality. The body criterion goes against immortality, barring the resurrection of the body. The concept of the immortality of the soul comes to us through Greek philosophy and religious sources. The careful discussion of the logical and metaphysical issues begins with Locke and the criticisms of Reid, and has continued in the present century with the elaboration of the so-called 'puzzle cases' of which Locke's case of the prince and the cobbler was the first.

Notes

1 By a principle called 'Leibniz's Law', which states that if x and y are identical, then whatever is true of x is true of y. This could be called the Identification Parade Principle. If the person I saw committing the crime was white and female, and all the persons in the line-up are black and male, then none of the persons in the line-up committed the crime.

2 But not perfect, because it cannot distinguish identical twins, who have the same genetic material – the DNA criterion would actually make them into the same person, which they obviously cannot be in any sense other than the most tenuous psychological one – and because of the question of reliability. A.J. Jeffreys has reported in *Nature* that through the DNA identification techniques '6% of identical twins were found to have nonidentical [DNA] patterns.' (This means that identical twins cannot simply be *excluded* from the DNA criterion.) The 6 per cent figure is 'a surprising finding, if confirmed, [because it] would suggest that identical twins are not identical, that identical twins become less identical over time, and/or that technical errors inherent in these methods are more common than is presently appreciated'. Paul R. Billings, 'Gene Technology: Views of its Criminal Justice Applications', in Paul R. Billings, ed., *DNA on Trial: Genetic Identification and Criminal Justice*, Plainview, N.Y., Cold Spring Harbor Laboratory Press, 1992, p. 3.

3 From Lorne T. Kirby, *DNA Fingerprinting*, New York, Macmillan, 1990, p. 22.

4 Anthony Quinton, 'The Soul', *Journal of Philosophy* LIX, No. 15 (1962), p. 394,

reprinted in John Perry, ed., *Personal Identity*, Berkeley, Calif., University of California Press, 1975, p. 54.

5 John Locke, *An Essay Concerning Human Understanding*, ed. Peter H. Nidditch, Oxford, Oxford University Press, 1975, p. 340.

6 Ibid.

7 Quinton, 'The Soul', in Perry, *Personal Identity*, p. 59; Derek Parfit, *Reasons and Persons*, Oxford, Oxford University Press, 1986, p. 206.

8 Thomas Reid, *Essays on the Intellectual Powers of Man*, Edinburgh, John Bell, 1785, p. 334.

9 Perry, *Personal Identity*, p. 19.

10 William L. Confer and Billie S. Ables, *Multiple Personality: Etiology, Diagnosis and Treatment*, New York, Human Science, 1983, p. 16.

11 Even for clocks and other artefacts which can survive *disassembly*. The point is that a clock cannot be killed, and so when it is disassembled nothing is lost except the organization of the parts. But since a clock *is* parts plus their organization, provided the organization is not lost, then the continuity of the parts even through disassembly is the continuity of the clock. For a brilliant discussion of the problems of artefact identity, see David Wiggins, *Substance and Sameness*, Oxford, Blackwell, 1980, pp. 90ff. In Wiggins' book, the similarity or community of properties, whether partial or complete, insisted on by the above analysis is a *consequence* of the real principle of identity, his D(ii), which says that identity of x with anything requires that x should *be something*, a man, a horse or a bus shelter, for example, throughout the time that it exists (p. 59), or that substance determines sameness, not the other way round.

12 See Parfit, *Reasons and Persons*, Part III, Ch. 10, for an extended discussion of teletransportation.

13 Ernst Mach, *The Analysis of Sensations and the Relation of the Physical to the Psychical*, trans. C.M. Williams, New York, Dover, 1959, p. 2.

Reading

H.P. Grice, 'Personal Identity', *Mind* 50 (1941), pp. 330–350.

David Hume, *A Treatise of Human Nature*, ed. L.A. Selby-Bigge, Oxford, Oxford University Press, 1888, Part IV, Book 1, Section 6.

John Locke, *An Essay Concerning Human Understanding*, ed. Peter H. Nidditch, Oxford, Oxford University Press, 1975, Ch. 27.

*John Perry, ed., *Personal Identity*, Berkeley, Calif., University of California Press, 1975.

Anthony Quinton, 'The Soul', *Journal of Philosophy* 59 (1962).

Thomas Reid, *Essays on the Intellectual Powers of Man*, Edinburgh, John Bell, 1785.

David Wiggins, *Substance and Sameness*, Oxford, Blackwell, 1980.

B.A.O. Williams, 'Personal Identity and Individuation', *Proceedings of the Aristotelian Society* 57 (1956–1957), pp. 229–252.

8
The Mind–Body Problem
How is the Mind Related to the Body?

A
The Problem

How are the mind and body related? This first approximation to a formulation of the mind–body problem will not do, both because it is too vague and because it does not express a problem but only a question. Consider the question, 'How is France related to Germany?' This question will call up at best a catalogue of official guidebook facts, unless there is some reason to suppose that there is a particular problem about the relationship between France and Germany, say a problem about trade or territory.

Consider the following propositions.

> The human body is physical.
> The human mind is non-physical.
> Mind and body interact.
> Physical and non-physical things do not interact.

This formulation of the mind–body problem is due to Keith Campbell.[1] He points out that the four propositions form an inconsistent tetrad. Any three are consistent, but any three imply that the fourth is false.

For example, suppose that the first three are true. Then the fourth must be false, as we are given in the third an example of a physical thing and a non-physical thing which *do* interact, namely the mind and the body.

Or suppose that the last three of Campbell's initial propositions are true. Then the human mind is non-physical but it does interact with the body. But physical and non-physical things don't interact. So the body can't be physical.

Confronted with this problem, most people pick on the fourth proposition to deny. After all, they reason, we *know* that physical and non-physical things do interact, because we have one good *example* of interaction, namely the interaction of mind and body, assuming of course that the human body is physical and the mind non-physical. The body interacts with the mind whenever we get drunk, for example. The physical presence of the beer in the body produces events in the mind, mental events, of confusion, mirth, depression or whatever. On the other hand, the mere *thought* of the beloved, something in the mind, can increase the pulse rate, and anxiety, which is mental or psychological, can cause palpitations and sweating.

How then can the fourth non-interactionist proposition possibly be affirmed? The answer lies in the understanding of the concepts of the physical and the non-physical. It will be convenient to use Campbell's initial propositions for this analysis. What does it come to to say the following?

The human body is physical.

Or, generalizing,

X is physical.

Suppose the following analysis.

↓

X has spatio-temporal location, volume and mass.

There are other physical magnitudes – velocity, for example – but for simplicity let us restrict attention to these three. Note that colour, smell and taste are not counted as physical by the definition given in the analysis.

Because the definition is an analysis, it says both that if X is physical, then X has spatio-temporal location, volume and mass, and that if X has spatio-temporal location, volume and mass, then it is physical. Taking this second implication, if X is *not* physical, then by *modus tollens* X does not have a spatio-temporal location, volume or mass.

And now a justification for the fourth proposition is starting to appear. How can something which *does* have a position in space and time affect something which does *not*, and vice versa? An analogy may help. Imagine some person at a fixed address (= a position in space) trying to send a letter to someone of no fixed address (= no position in space). The letter can be written all right, but how will the envelope be addressed? 'Fred Bloggs,

Esq., Address Unknown'? Such a letter would be *returned*, and probably not even marked 'address unknown' by the Post Office, because it is already so marked by the addressee. And even if it is in some manner addressed, how will it be delivered, as there is nowhere (no *'where?'*) to which it can be delivered? With persons of no fixed address one can some-times assume an *approximate* address, e.g. 'somewhere in South Croy-don', and then perhaps try several Post Office Box locations within this general area. But here there actually *is* a general location, though of greater area.

Again, if something has no spatial and temporal location, how then can it act on something which does? If, at any particular time, a person is at no place, how then can she act on something which *is* in a place? If she sticks out her leg to trip someone up in South Croydon, for example, how will her foot, which has no location, suddenly manifest itself in South Croy-don? And if she acts at no time, how is this different from not acting at all?

Taking just spatial location as the key property which distinguishes the physical from the non-physical, as Descartes did in the original formula-tion of the mind–body problem,[2] we have at least a strong set of intuitive considerations which support the fourth proposition.

The Problem of Sensations

We know that conscious visual perception occurs when light enters the eye from the perceived object. The light stimulates the retina, and an electrochemical impulse is sent down the optic nerve. This impulse is a message which travels to the occipital cortex, the locus of vision in the central nervous sys-tem. The result is the conscious perception, a mental event. But how do the events in the occipital cortex cause a conscious per-ception, if the perception, being mental, does *not* have a spatial location, and the cortical events do? (This is the South Croydon problem.) How is the conscious perception, which is a mental event, related to its cortical causes, which are physical events? When a surgeon examines the brain of a patient, there is never any observable thing which could be called a 'conscious percep-tion'. No matter how far into the brain the surgeon goes, he or she will never find this mental event. For the question, *'Where is the perception located?'* involves a failure to grasp the non-spatiality of the mental.

The Problem of Volitions

There is a similar problem going in the opposite direction from inner thoughts and volitions to outer physical acts. How does a non-physical thought, unlocated and unlocatable, make my arm move? One would expect the thought so to speak to *pass through* the solid arm, if sent in its direction. Perhaps the thought works on the muscles, which in turn move the arm. One would expect the thought so to speak to *pass through* the solid muscles. How can a thought move muscles? Perhaps it does so by sending an electrochemical impulse from the brain. But then the same problem exists. How does the mind cause the brain to produce electrochemical signals? This would be every bit as extraordinary a thing as the mind initiating chemical reactions in a test-tube with no physical contact. It would be telekinesis. But then how can the mind have *physical contact* with *anything*, including the brain, since thought is non-physical? Any such contact would be telekinetic. If what makes the mind unable to affect a test-tube full of organic chemicals on a laboratory bench is the fact that the test-tube and its organic chemicals are physical, how can the mind pull off the same trick with the brain, which is just as physical as the test-tube and its contents? This is the problem of volitions.

Having seen the rationale for the fourth proposition, suspicion will be bound to fall on the second of Campbell's initial propositions. What reasons can be given for thinking that the mind is non-physical?

Given the above analysis of the physical, we would expect mental things, like conscious afterimage perceptions, or thoughts, and the mind in general, to have the proper physical characteristics. But:

> The mass of a conscious afterimage perception of a pink spot is M.

or:

> The spatial location of a conscious afterimage perception of a pink spot is L, in the occipital cortex.

are propositions which cannot be true. No matter where the surgeon looks in the patient's brain for the afterimage, he or she will apprehend neither the conscious afterimage perception of the pink spot which the patient does, nor the pink spot itself, the afterimage. How then can the mass M or inertia of the spot be measured, or its weight in a gravitational field? How will the centroid or centre of mass of the afterimage be determined? Maybe the afterimage can be determined to have acceleration, across the visual field, but not so-called 'pure translation', which is the parallel motion of every particle in it. For there are no particles in it, as it does not exist in the brain, or any 'where?' else.

The same thing applies even more strongly to thoughts.

> The centre of mass of the thought that I am late for dinner is at x.

or:

> The spatial location of the thought that I am late for dinner is a place O, and O is 1.46 inches inside my skull.

If they have meaning, the last four propositions about mass, spatial location and centroid are false. Their meaning, however, if they have one, is very unclear indeed. But it is not as if we had scoured the brain for the thought that I am late for dinner, found it, and determined that its centre of mass is *not* at x. For we know that we have no idea even what it would amount to to find a thought in the brain or anywhere else, lying on the pavement or tucked into a suitcase. Even if we succeeded, how would we know it? Nor can we imagine any procedure for subjecting the thought that I am late for dinner to acceleration, and then considering the resulting resistance, and determining the centre of the parallel forces, the centre of gravity. So we know that the propositions ascribing physical characteristics to mental items cannot be true, either because they are meaningless or because they are false, in advance of any empirical investigation. For suppose that we did find a pink spot in the brain, and did determine its centroid. How could we tell that *this* was one and the same spot as the spot which the patient was 'seeing' as the afterimage? The situation is so unclear that even if every time we were to wiggle the spot the patient reported that his pink spot was wiggling, this would still not establish that the pink spot we were seeing was the very one he was seeing. All that would be established was that he was systematically getting information about what was happening to our pink spot. He might, for example, be seeing *the other end* of a rigid pink *rod* of which our spot was a cross-section!

We have considered a Cartesian definition of the physical, spatial location, which implies a corresponding feature of the non-physical, namely non-(spatial location). But this does not positively characterize that species of the non-physical which is the mental. How did Descartes accomplish this? His answer to the question of the defining characteristics of the mental was the following equation of the mental and the conscious.

> X is mental.
> ↓
> X is conscious.

Descartes also gave arguments for other criteria of the mental, for example the Platonic criterion of indivisibility as contrasted with the divisibility of matter. But it was immediately obvious to him, and to his critics, that his analysis of the mental as the conscious ruled out mental life in apparently unconscious states, for example during dreamless sleep. This was a problem, as Descartes identified *self* with *consciousness*. His answer to the counterexample was to say that in such cases we simply *forget* the conscious episodes when we wake up. It would be much simpler to say, as his critic Leibniz did, that there is such a thing as unconscious mental life. A familiar modern example would be the phenomenon of automatic or unconscious driving, in which many decisions and thoughts occur, of which the driver is not conscious, and is very surprised to 'wake up' and not know where she is. Has she really just forgotten her otherwise conscious experiences up the road? Another example is the startling ability of some people to set themselves a problem before they go to bed, and to produce the solution on waking. The only reasonable explanation is that unconscious thinking takes place during the night, not, as Descartes thought, that conscious thinking about the problem takes place, but all of it is forgotten, except the solution.

B
Some Proposed Solutions

Most of the serious contemporary solutions to the mind–body problem are different ways of denying the proposition that the human mind is non-physical, and yet not falling into the absurdities of propositions ascribing physical predicates to mental objects. These solutions include:

1 behaviourism, which flourished in the early and middle part of the twentieth century, especially in Britain and America;
2 central-state materialism, which replaced behaviourism, and found a special place in the hearts and minds of Australian and American philosophers in the fifties and sixties;
3 functionalism, due to the American philosopher Hilary Putnam, which replaced central-state materialism as a live option in the sixties and seventies;
4 eliminative materialism, which solves the mind–body problem by eliminating the mind in favour of the relevant part of the body described by means of cognitive science.

The four doctrines are materialistic or physicalistic because they deny that the mind is an example of something which lies beyond the physical. They deny this because they are typically part of a wider view of the world in which nothing at all lies beyond the physical.

The background to the four theories, however, lies far back in European philosophy, in the doctrine called dualism, which was Descartes' solution to the mind–body problem. Dualism deserves our respect, if only because for a problem as hard as the mind–body problem is, it would be unwise to dismiss out of hand any significant solution, especially the one given by the philosopher who first formulated the problem.

Dualism is the view that mind and body are distinct substances, in the sense that each can exist independently of the other. The mind, according to Descartes, is a non-physical or spiritual substance, and the body is a physical substance. The big problem for dualism in this sense is how the mind and body interact. Descartes' own answer was that the location of the interaction was the pineal gland in the brain, but it is easy to see that this does not solve the problem. If we cannot explain how the mind can interact with the body in general, or with the brain, for the reasons given above, how then can it interact with the pineal gland? For if the mind does not have a location in space, how can it affect the pineal gland, which has a very definite location? Descartes' dualism is called 'interactionist', because he took the view that the two substances do interact.

A different and non-interactionist dualist view is 'psychophysical parallelism', held by Leibniz, which states that mind and body do not interact in the sense that anything like a physical property is transmitted from one to the other, but that their actions are synchronized from the start, like two clocks keeping time together, which are set to strike at the same time. This view is distinct from the view known as 'occasionalism', another seventeenth-century doctrine, in which the striking of one clock (= the bodily event) is the *occasion* for God to cause the second clock to strike (= the mental event) and vice versa. Parallelism denies that the mental event and the physical event are at bottom two different kinds of substance. It does so by denying the proposition that the human body is physical. Leibniz's analysis of matter was that it is merely a 'phenomenon', though one which is 'well founded' in the sense that it expresses regular laws of behaviour. He did not believe in the existence of physical atoms, but only spiritual or non-physical ones.

In Descartes' view we are acquainted with our own consciousness, and this acquaintance is private. The fact that someone is aware of her or his own consciousness does not imply that anyone else is. This has been dubbed 'privileged access', and it is a part of the dualist theory. There is, however, a serious question as to whether the items which privileged access is access to are as clearly conceived as they need to be before the concept of privileged access makes sense.

How does the philosophical problem about mental processes and states and about behaviourism arise? – The first step is the one that altogether escapes notice. We talk of processes and states and leave their nature undecided. Sometime perhaps we shall know more about them – we think. But that is just what commits us to a particular way of looking at the matter. For we have a definite concept of what it means to know a process better. (The decisive move in the conjuring trick has been made, and it was the very one we thought quite innocent.)[3]

Wittgenstein is saying that we *accept* the proposition that the human mind is non-physical, and leave open the question of what the correct analysis of the proposition is. 'Sometime perhaps we shall know more about' what a non-physical state or process is, beyond the fact that we have direct and private access to it. And here a powerful false picture obtrudes. It is the picture of a person in 'a mental state', say anxiety and affection. The picture represents him or her, perhaps standing on a street corner, thinking affectionately of his or her friend, and anxiously awaiting the friend's coming. Floating above the person on the street corner is a bubble labelled 'anxiety', and another, labelled 'affection'. The person's mental states are these bubbles. Then comes the question, 'What is a bubble?' The bubbles, independent of their content, are the things whose 'nature' we leave 'undecided', thinking that only in this nature is the secret of what the non-physical and the mental are. Only the person (and the artist!) can see what is in his or her own bubble. He or she has 'privileged access' to its contents, his or her own private conscious states.

Wittgenstein's attack on the idea of the private conscious mental state came to be called 'the private language argument', and was given particular force in his justly celebrated image of the beetle in the box.

If I say of myself that it is only from my own case that I know what the word 'pain' means – must I not say the same of other people too? And how can I generalize the *one* case so irresponsibly?

Now someone tells me that *he* knows what pain is only from his own case! – Suppose everyone had a box with something in it: we call it a 'beetle'. No one can look into anyone else's box, and everyone says he knows what a beetle is only by looking at *his* beetle. – Here it would be quite possible for everyone to have something different in his box. One might even imagine such a thing constantly changing. – But suppose the word 'beetle' has a use in these people's language? – If so it would not be used as the name of a thing. The thing in the box has no

place in the language-game at all; not even as a *something*: for
the box might even be empty. – No, one can 'divide through'
by the thing in the box; it cancels out, whatever it is.

That is to say: if we construe the grammar of the expression
of sensation on the model of 'object and designation' the object
drops out of consideration as irrelevant.[4]

Behaviourism

Wittgenstein is sometimes accused of being a 'behaviourist', that is, of
believing that the analysis of mental states in general and intelligent mental states in particular is to be given in terms of intelligent *behaviour*.
What Wittgenstein says, however, is that *if* we understand the grammar of
mental terms, like 'thought', on the model of 'object and designation', *then*
the mental 'object drops out of consideration as irrelevant', and all that is
left is the behaviour. Wittgenstein is at one with the behaviourists in
thinking that the thing in the box is not a *something*. But the behaviourists also tended to think of it as a *nothing* as well. '"And yet you again
and again reach the conclusion that the sensation itself is a *nothing*." – Not
at all. It is not a *something*, but not a nothing either!'[5]

To this observation, Wittgenstein adds, 'The conclusion [he means to
the beetle in the box argument] was only that a nothing would serve just
as well as a something about which nothing could be said. We have only
rejected the grammar which tries to force itself on us here.' How is it
possible to deny this grammar or the claim that words for sensations name
mental states, which are the sensations themselves?

The answer of the behaviourists was that mental states are not invisible
internal objects, but external activities and dispositions to engage in these
activities. Dispositions are of course invisible, but they are not internal.
The word 'anger', for example, according to the behaviourists, does not
name an inner mental state, accessible only to the angry person. To say
that an angry person is angry is not to say that she or he is afflicted with
an inner mental state of anger, but rather that she or he is engaging in
angry *behaviour*.

S is angry.
↓
S engages in angry behaviour.

People can be angry, however, when they show no behavioural sign of
being angry, so this analysis needs amending. The behaviourists solved
the problem with the concept of a *disposition* or a tendency. A pane of

glass, to use the stock example, is called 'brittle' if it breaks or cracks easily. But it can be brittle even when it is not actually breaking. We say it has a *disposition* to crack. This means that *if* it were hit, and not even very hard, it would crack. This truth obtains even if it is *not* hit, which seems mysterious. (How it is possible is what philosophers call 'the problem of counterfactual conditionals'. What is the *fact* corresponding to the truth of the 'if it were hit'?) Similarly, the behaviourists argued, an angry person has a disposition to engage in angry behaviour, even if the disposition is not manifested at any particular time.

↓

S engages in angry behaviour or is disposed to engage in angry behaviour.

This analysis will still not quite do, as it contains the word 'angry', which is, along with the words 'S' and 'is', exactly what the analysis is supposed to be an analysis of.

One obvious answer to this objection is to substitute for 'angry behaviour' a lengthy disjunctive description along the lines of 'shakes her or his fist, or shouts, or accuses someone of something, or stamps her or his foot . . . ' and so on.

↓

S shakes her or his fist, or shouts, or accuses someone of something, or stamps her or his foot, or grinds her or his teeth or . . .

But the three little dots, meaning 'and so on', introduce a further problem, which makes the whole behaviourist analysis unravel. How many different ways are there of expressing anger? Could one, for example, include forgiving one's enemy as a form of anger? Mostly not, if the forgiveness is genuine, because angry people are typically unforgiving, but some subtle and malicious individual psychologies do unconsciously use forgiveness as an instrument of anger. Or one could include blinking one's eyes as a form of angry behaviour, which in some cases it is, though a small minority of cases. Or, it has been argued, some people more or less consciously divert and convert their anger into some form of otherwise inexplicable illness. It has been argued that endogenous depression is a form of repressed anger. If this is so, depressed behaviour must be included on the list.

This problem is known as the problem of multiple responses. There seem to be indefinitely many different ways of expressing anger in behaviour, which will vary wildly from culture to culture. Could there be a culture in which stamping the foot was a form of affectionate *greeting*? If

so, the analysis is immediately derailed. For we have an example of someone stamping her or his foot who is not angry. How then is the analysis
ever to be completed? One could add on to the analysis a 'closing clause',
thus:

↓

S shakes her or his fist, or shouts, or accuses someone of something, or stamps her or his foot, or grinds her or his teeth, or
engages in other *angry* behaviour.

Here again, the very term to be analysed, 'angry', pops up in the analysis. Without the closing clause the analysis is incomplete, but with it the
analysis is circular.

I conclude that behaviourism is false.

On one crucial point the behaviourists were agreed with Wittgenstein.
In Wittgenstein's words, terms for mental states are not to be construed on
the model of 'designator' and 'object'. For, according to the behaviourist,
there *are* no mental objects. There are rather tendencies to physical
behaviour. So the behaviourists reject the proposition that 'The human
mind is non-physical' because the mind boils down to behaviour, which is
not an 'object', and behaviour is physical.

Central-state materialism

Going on to our second proposed solution, the central-state materialists
take the view that mental states are states of the brain, or the central
nervous system, or that the mind *is* the brain. The term 'central-state' is
used to distinguish these materialists from the behaviourists, who could be
'peripheral-state' materialists, the peripheral states in question being
behaviour. So the central-state materialists reject the proposition that the
human mind is non-physical for a different reason. The behaviourist says
in effect that there is no such *object* as the mind, because it is at bottom
human *activity* or *behaviour*. Hence there is no non-physical object called
the human mind. The central-state materialist believes by contrast that
there *is* such a thing as the human mind, but that, since it is the brain, it is
not non-physical but physical.

S is in mental state m.
↓
S is in brain state b.

Taking the mind as the sum of mental states, and generalizing, we have the denial of Campbell's initial proposition that the human mind is non-physical, assuming that brain states are non-physical.

This new neurophysiological analysis is something of a promissory note, however, as not nearly all mental states have been correlated with specific and named brain states. So there is the possibility that all brain states will come to be tabulated and numbered, and all mental states assigned a particular numbered brain state, but that some particular and not even very recherché mental state, for example narrow-mindedness, just turns out not to have a brain 'address'. Whether this will transpire is surely a matter of empirical fact if anything is, so it should not be ruled out *a priori* by a scientific philosophy.

Central-state materialists does not wish to argue that, in English, 'mental state' *means* 'brain state', that is, they do not wish to argue that the identity of mental state and brain state is a conceptual or *a priori* affair. The identity in the *Identity Theory*, as central-state materialism has been called, because it asserts the identity of mind and brain, is, according to its adherents, an *empirical* identity. That is, it is an identity whose truth is an empirical discovery, unlike the identity of triangles and three-sided figures. So central-state materialism is *not* committed to the following analysis.

S has a narrow mind.
↓
S has a narrow brain.

In the Identity Theory the mental state 'having a narrow mind' does not reduce to the anatomical brain state 'being narrow', but to some other neurophysiological state, a hypothesized set of neurons firing in a characteristic pattern. 'Being narrow' would be the wrong choice of brain state in the theory, as there is obviously no correlation between the macrostructure of the brain and the 'shape' or state of the mind. So the Identity Theory denies that the *word* 'mind' means 'brain'. For if it were conceded that it did, the theory would be stuck with the substitution of the 'brain' for 'mind', and with the absurd proposition that a narrow mind means a narrow brain. At the same time it maintains that the mind is as a matter of empirical fact the brain, just as, in one of the examples favoured by central-state materialists, the word 'gene' does not *mean* the same thing as the phrase 'DNA molecule', or it would not have been an empirical discovery that the gene is the DNA molecule.

The distinction (between what the word 'mind' means – not 'brain' – and what it happens to refer to) enables the Identity Theory to meet various important objections. For example, the criticism has been made of the Identity Theory that we can talk about our mental states and yet know nothing about our brain states. So the two cannot be identical. But then we might equally well know quite a lot about the genes without knowing anything about the DNA molecule.[6]

There is another more damaging line of criticism of the Identity Theory, outlined by David Armstrong in Chapter 6 of *A Materialist Theory of Mind*.[7] The argument goes like this.

(1) 'The mind is the brain' is a *contingent* identity statement, unlike 'The number three is the whole number which lies between two and four.'

(2) With contingent identity statements of the form 'x is y', it must be possible to give an independent explanation of the meaning of the terms 'x' and 'y' or independently identify x and y. With a necessary identity statement like 'The number three is the whole number which lies between two and four', in explaining what 'the number three' is, we have also thereby inadvertently explained what 'the number which lies between two and four' is.

(3) How is the term 'mind' to be explained independently of 'brain'? The mind is identified, says Armstrong, as the *effect* of stimuli, namely sensations, and the *cause* of behaviour, which is volitions.

> S is in a mental state m.
> ↓
> S is in a physical state p which is caused by stimuli and causes behaviour.

This is Armstrong's analysis. The state p is further identified empirically with the state of the central nervous system p.

(4) Yet there are states which cause behaviour which are not mental. An example is the cause of a reflex knee jerk.[8] So the analysis must be amended to read:

> S is in a physical state p which is caused by stimuli and causes *behaviour proper*.

The point of the amendment is that by 'behaviour proper' Armstrong means behaviour which is not just a physical action of the body or 'physical behaviour'. But this 'not just' implies a relationship to the mind and to mental states. To behave in such a way as to move one's leg is to do so *intentionally*, which is to be in the state of *mind* 'intending to move one's leg'. So we have:

> S is in a physical state p which is caused by stimuli and which causes that kind of behaviour which S engages in when *S is in a mental state m*.

The analysis is circular, as the final proposition contains the initial proposition to be analysed. The situation is even worse for central-state materialism, as Armstrong presents it, in the case of the physical states which are caused by stimuli. For no doubt there are huge numbers of physical states caused by stimuli which are not mental, ranging from blinking one's eyes as a result of getting sand in them to catching a cold. How are these to be distinguished from what could be called 'stimuli proper', that is, perceptual or mental ones?[9]

So   (5)   The Identity Theory is false.

There were other difficulties with the Identity Theory. Perhaps the biggest was what came to be seen as a sort of parochialism or anthropocentrism. If mental state m is brain state b, then no one can be in mental state m who cannot be in brain state b. So unless Martians have a physiology identical to ours, they cannot be angry or sad. They cannot be thinking out the problem 'What is 7×9?' unless their neurophysiology works the problem in exactly the same way as ours. This problem has been called the multiple instantiation problem. There are just too many different ways of instantiating the thinking out of an arithmetical or any other problem, not all of them even physiological.

It came to seem as if the identity theorist was insisting that the mental state of calculating the product of 7 and 9 could only be a single physical state, or could only be achieved by one physical state. With the advent of powerful computers able to perform a variety of at least mental-like activities, from playing chess to doing college calculus, it also came to seem obvious that being in a mental state was not a matter of being in a physical state, but rather of being in what was called a *functional* or *computational* state. It makes no odds whether a computer is made of vacuum tubes or bits of string or wire or printed circuits or beads. Provided it runs the same program for solving '$7 \times 9 = ?$', and no matter what it is made of, it is in the same functional state as any other machine trying to solve the same problem. The view which identifies mental states with functional states rather than physical states, and makes mentality a matter of form rather than matter, is called *functionalism*.

Functionalism

Functionalism more or less killed the Identity Theory, not only by direct logical refutation, but also by being more exciting and relating in a more interesting way to the emerging field of cognitive science, which is a mixture of philosophy, physiology, computer studies and artificial intelligence, experimental psychology and theoretical linguistics. Part of the attractiveness of the theory came from the naturalness and power of the analogy of computer hardware with the brain and the computer software or program with mental activity. The analogy seemed to provide just the right kind of distinction between mind and body to explain the insight of dualism without allowing its problems. The functionalist can be taken to be arguing that the human mind is just as physical as a computer program, but also that it embodies non-physical properties or states, namely functional ones.

It is a remarkable fact that functionalism ran into exactly the same *kind* of difficulty as behaviourism and central-state materialism had. Just like them, it was unable to reproduce the variety and complexity of a particular named mental state in its preferred reductive formula. Hilary Putnam, who had himself discovered functionalism in the sixties, came to reject it for this very reason.

> In sum, not only is it false that different humans are in one and the same computational state whenever they believe that there are a lot of cats in the neighborhood, or whatever, but members of different physically possible species who are sufficiently similar in their linguistic behaviour in a range of environments to permit us to translate some of their utterances as meaning 'there are a lot of cats in the neighborhood,' or whatever, may have computational states that lie in an incomparable 'space' of computational states. Even if their way of reasoning in some situations is 'similar' to ours (when we view them with the aid of some translation manual that we succeed in constructing), this does not imply that the states or the algorithm are the same. The idea that there is *one* computational state that every being who believes that there are a lot of cats in the neighborhood (or whatever) *must* be in is false . . . The reason for introducing functionalism in the first place was precisely that we are not going to find any physical state (other than one defined by the sort of 'infinite list' that we ruled out as 'cheating') that all

physically possible believers have to be in to have a given belief, or whatever. But now it emerges that the same thing is true of computational states. And (finite) conjunctions, disjunctions, etc., of physical and computational states will not help either. Physically possible sentient beings just come in too many 'designs', physically and computationally speaking, for anything like 'one computational state per propositional attitude' functionalism to be true.[10]

The three solutions to the mind–body problem so far discussed (behaviourism, central-state materialism and functionalism) share one crucial defect. This is what I shall call the problem of absent sense-data (it is usually called the absent *qualia* problem, but for our purpose sense-data and *qualia* can be taken to be the same things). The problem could also be extended, and the quotation from Putnam above can be read from this point of view, to apply not just to sense-data but to all 'data' or units of information, such as the data of the facts of propositional attitudes.

The general problem is this. It is perfectly *possible* for an organism, a person even, to have a certain behavioural disposition, or to be in a certain brain state, or to be in a corresponding functional state, *without having the conscious experience* or the sense-data which form the mental state. Thus an organism could be such as to be disposed to cry 'red' (a behavioural disposition) or to have neurons x, y, z . . . firing, or be in the functional state which leads to 'red-sensitive' behaviour (depending on which of these philosophies of mind is chosen) *without any apprehension of the colour red*!

The so-called problem of spectrum inversion makes roughly the same point. We are to imagine that someone, let us say poor old S again, has her or his colour sense-data systematically inverted, so that the reds she or he previously saw are replaced by the blue-greens, and vice versa, the yellows by the violets, and vice versa, the blacks by the whites, and vice versa, and so on. Now S's mental states are systematically switched. If this is possible, it is surely *possible* that at the same time S's behaviour dispositions, or her or his brain activity, or her or his functional states, are unaltered. It follows that mental states cannot *be* any of these things. What absent sense-data and spectrum inversion imply is something which we already knew from the previous criticisms: that the behaviourist, central-state materialist and functionalist analyses are false. They miss the phenomena of mind, the common facts available to anyone who can *see* the colour red or does not *believe* in God or *knows* that he does not *intend* to pay his brother back.

Eliminative materialism

The conviction that this conclusion is correct is reinforced by the claim made by the fourth of our solutions to the mind–body problem, eliminative materialism, which can be regarded as the final development, a sort of vanishing act, of theories in the same line as behaviourism, central-state materialism and functionalism. The eliminative materialists despaired, like Putnam, of finding an analysis of mental states described in terms of everyday or commonsense psychological concepts or propositional attitudes such as belief, desire, intention and so on. The theory of eliminativism proposed to purge scientific and psychological theory of such concepts, comparing them to concepts like *witch* and *demon*, which were also at one time commonly accepted. That is, not finding one physical state or any other kind of state corresponding to the concept *belief*, just as no one real empirically discoverable state corresponded to *witch*, eliminativism took the line that the concept of belief was itself at fault, and all the other ordinary psychological concepts as well. 'Believe' is an incoherent concept, eliminativists believe (oops!). Anyway, this is what they *argue*. Eliminativism says that everyday psychological concepts will be replaced by those concepts which cognitive science uses – or will use – in its explanations of human behaviour and cognition, or that they should be replaced. Like astrology and the witch theory, the concepts of 'folk psychology' are held to embody a false theory. That theory is destined to be replaced by the true scientific one,[11] just as the concept *witch* has been replaced by something like *unpopular crone who talks to herself and curses the neighbours*.

Can one be forgiven for concluding as a result that there is something to be said for the proposition that the mind is non-physical after all, and that it must be one, or more, of Campbell's other initial propositions which is false? The alternative is to solve the mind–body problem by denying the existence of the mind as ordinarily characterized, and to make our ordinary lives and experience as ordinarily characterized unintelligible from the higher scientific conception. Most people would – quite rightly – jib at this.

The view which I wish to examine next, neutral monism, is an old-fashioned theory, dating from the turn of the century, which denies the final truth of this 'higher' scientific point of view.

C
Neutral Monism

The first of Campbell's initial propositions says that the human body is physical. In this final section on the mind–body problem I wish tentatively to endorse a solution, or anyway part of one version of it, which denies the proposition that mind and body interact, a theory known as 'neutral monism.' The theory was held at different times by the late nineteenth- and twentieth-century philosophers Ernst Mach, William James, Bertrand Russell, A.J. Ayer and, according to a recent book, throughout his life by Ludwig Wittgenstein.[12] It is the view that mind and body, and bodies or matter generally, are constructions from neutral data which are themselves neither mental nor physical.

These neutral data are given various different names by the different philosophers who have subscribed to neutral monism. 'Sense-data', 'sensations' and 'elements' are the most common. Mach gives as his choice of elements, 'colors, sounds, temperatures, pressures, spaces, times, and so forth',[13] as well as 'dispositions of mind, feelings, and volitions'.[14] He labels the group of elements we call 'bodies' $A\ B\ C\ldots$; our own body, $K\ L\ M\ldots$; and the complex of volitions, memory-images, and the rest, we shall represent by $\alpha\ \beta\ \gamma$.[15]

Mach describes various interesting and important relations between these complexes. For example, the elements $K\ L\ M\ \ldots$ tend to repeat themselves in association with all other $A\ B\ C\ldots$ Also $\alpha\ \beta\ \gamma\ \ldots$ tend to be more unstable and evanescent than $A\ B\ C\ldots$ In addition, 'My body differs from other human bodies ... by the circumstance, that it is only seen piecemeal, and, especially, it is seen without a head.'[16] $A\ B\ C\ldots$ 'stand in a relation of quite peculiar dependence to certain of the elements $K\ L\ M -$ the nerves of our own body, namely – by which the facts of sensory physiology are expressed'.[17] 'A magnet in our neighborhood disturbs the particles of iron near it; a falling boulder shakes the earth; but the severing of a nerve sets in motion the *whole* system of elements.'[18]

The elements $A\ B\ C\ldots$, $K\ L\ M\ldots$ and $\alpha\ \beta\ \gamma\ldots$ are, taken individually, neither mental nor physical. They become physical when they have a place in a stable grouping of elements, or mental when they belong along with a group of other 'unstable' elements. A patch of colour, for example, all by itself, does not have a volume or a spatial location. To other patches of colour, however, it stands in various spatial relations.

> A color is a physical object as soon as we consider its dependencies, for instance, upon its luminous source, upon other colors, upon temperatures, upon spaces, and so forth. When we consider, however, its dependence upon the retina (the elements $K\ L\ M\ldots$) it is a psychological object, a sensation. Not the subject-matter, but the direction of our investigation, is different in the two domains.[19]

Bertrand Russell illustrated this point with a celebrated comparison between two different kinds of postal directory, a geographical or street directory and an alphabetical one.[20] The same names appear in both directories, but in a different order and with different relations to the other names. Taken by itself, no element, consisting of a name, address and telephone number, is either 'alphabetical' – mental, in Russell's simile – or 'geographical' – physical. All the elements of the two directories are 'neutral'. Hence the 'neutral' in 'neutral monism'.

Consider an alphabetical directory.

Aardvark, Kate and Fred, Animal Towers, Flat 3	233-2420
Ant, Anthony, 23 Bug Lane	233-2421
Antelope, Sir Robert, 8 Horn Street	Ex directory

These entries will also appear in a complete street directory. Anthony Ant's listing, for example, will be found in the street directory under Bug Lane, along with the other Bug Lane entries.

Ladybird, Lucy, 22 Bug Lane	237-1111
Ant, Anthony, 23 Bug Lane	233-2421
Bumblebee, Carol Scott, 24 Bug Lane	236-2478

An entry given by itself and not in the context of either list, such as 'Ant, Anthony, 23 Bug Lane, 233–2421', would be neutral in the sense that it is neither alphabetical nor geographical.

Returning to Mach's view, the elements of the complex which I call my own body, $K\ L\ M \ldots$, which we can call B, the body without a head, are physical only because they are placed in relation to other physical elements in the group $A\ B\ C \ldots$. If B is taken in relation to my blinking, it becomes mental, an element β, say. This means that in Mach's view the proposition that 'The human body is physical' is not true of B as a neutral element, and as such B does not have spatial location and volume, the first two properties given in the analysis of 'physical' above, any more than any other isolated image. Mach did not in fact believe that mass is a true characteristic of the physical. He thought that mass was actually a function of acceleration.

How does Mach's interesting view solve the problem of sensations, given earlier?

We see an object having a point S. If we touch S, that is, if we bring it into connection with our own bodies, we receive a prick. We can see S without feeling the prick. But as soon as we feel the prick we find S on the skin. The visible point, therefore, is annexed, according to circumstances, as something accidental. From the frequency of analogous occurrences we ultimately accustom ourselves to regard all properties of bodies as 'effects' proceeding from permanent nuclei and conveyed to the ego through the medium of the body, which effects we call sensations.[21]

The point is that S is also a sensation, and so what we have is not the observation of a physical point S followed by a mental sensation, but one element followed by another, the former classified as physical, on this occasion, and the latter as mental.

How does an element like S relate to the body, $K L M \ldots$, or to those elements of it which constitute the brain? The question can be taken in two distinct and different ways, depending on whether S is regarded as mental or as physical.

If S is physical, then one is treating oneself like any other physical observer, and asking how S is related to the brain. The answer is that it is to the left of the brain, say, two feet away from it, slightly below it, has such-and-such an effect on it, and so on.

On the other hand if S is taken as a mental element, part of $a \beta \gamma \ldots$, then it is one of those intermittent and unstable elements in my sensations. How is it related to the sensation of the brain, another such mental element? The answer is that it is not, because I do not have a sensation of my brain! (Mine, remember, is the body without a head.)

The mind–body problem, on this analysis, comes from *confusing* the two series of the mental and the physical, and trying either (1) to locate a mental item, the sensation S, in a physical series, where it does not exist or belong, or (2) to locate a physical item, the brain, in a mental series, where it does not exist or belong.

If I am observing you and your brain physically, there *is* no sensation of S in the series I observe. There is of course my *own* sensation of S, but the problem of sensations does not concern the relation of *my* sensation to *your* brain. If on the other hand I am observing my own mental series of sensations, then the problem of the relation of S to the brain does not arise either, as there is no sensation of the brain or of anything physical.

Rather surprisingly, perhaps, the false picture behind the problem of sensations and the mind–body problem generally is the picture of the causal chain from (1) the reflection of light into the eye through (2) stimulation of the retina, through (3) the optic nerve, to (4) the visual cortex, and on to (5) the conscious sensation. This picture muddles up four Machian elements in a physical series (1)–(4) with one (5) from a mental series. As A.J. Ayer observes:[22]

If there seems to be a mystery in this case, it is because we are misled by our conceptual systems; not by the facts themselves

but by the pictures by which we interpret the facts. The physi-
ologist's story is complete in itself. The characters that figure in
it are nerve cells, electrical impulses, and so forth. It has no place
for an entirely different cast, of sensations, thoughts, feelings,
and the other *personae* of the mental play. And just because it
has no place for them they do not intervene in it. The muddle
arises from trying to make them intervene, as I am afraid Lord
Samuel does. [23] We then get a confused, indeed an unintelligible, story of electrical impulses being transmuted into sensations, or of mental processes interleaved with disturbances of
the nervous cells. The picture we are given is that of messengers
travelling through the brain, reaching a mysterious entity
called the mind, receiving orders from it, and then travelling on.
But since the mind has no position in space – it is by definition
not the sort of thing that can have a position in space – it does
not literally make sense to talk of physical signals reaching it;
nor are there such temporal gaps in the procession of nervous
impulses as would leave room for mental characters to intervene. In short, the two stories will not mix. It is like trying to
play *Hamlet*, not without the Prince of Denmark, but with Peri-
cles, Prince of Tyre. Each is an interpretation of certain
phenomena and they are connected by the fact that, in certain
conditions, when one of them is true, the other is true also.

It is commonly thought that neutral monism is a solution to the mind–
body problem or is intended as a solution to the mind–body problem.
Neither is the case. The truth is that neutral monism is the setting for such
a solution, the one Ayer gives which demonstrates that the mind–body
problem is a muddle, not a mystery, but is not itself the solution. Neutral
monism asserts that the series of data identified as mind and the series of
data identified as body are constructions. The solution to the mind–body
problem is to be found in the resulting but distinct insight that the two
stories will not mix, as Ayer puts it.

Consider a set of 100 photographs of the objects in a room. Let some of
the photographs be taken from the ceiling, some from the floor, some from
behind bits of furniture, and some from the centre of the room. Let some
be taken towards the light, others away from it, and let some be over-
exposed or underexposed, or damaged during development.

We can select a series of relatively stable elements from these data. Call
these 'physical' elements. They are the ones which can be identified in
more than one photograph, such as pieces of furniture. Let the elements
which are unstable, in the sense that they occur in only one or a few
photographs, be called 'mental' elements. Let one photograph, perhaps

achieved by a reflection in the window, be of the camera itself. And let the camera be so constructed that it always photographs an obtruding part of itself.

Now we can ask the question how the 'mental' elements in the photographs can 'arise' from any photographed 'physical' elements, in particular from those elements which form part of the camera. And there will be no answer! The mental 'effects' cannot be derived from any transformation of any of the bodily physical elements in the photographs, and none of the behaviour of the 'bodily' elements can be derived from the 'mental' elements. There is here then *a mind–body problem to be found in the behaviour of the data from a recording device* with no miraculous mental or physical properties.

Ayer's point that 'the two stories will not mix' can be further illustrated with another model of Mach's neutral elements which I have derived for the purpose. Let there be a series of numerals, representing the natural numbers from one to seven, each numeral coloured one of the main spectral colours red (R), orange (O), yellow (Y), green (G), blue (B), violet (V) or indigo (I). Let these coloured numerals, rather like the numbers often seen on kitchen refrigerators, represent Mach's elements, and imagine them distributed randomly, thus.

$$2$$
$$7$$
$$6$$
$$5 \qquad 4$$
$$1$$
$$3$$

Suppose the colours of the numerals are as follows:

   1–O 2-G 3-Y 4-B 5-R 7-I 6-V

We can now order the unordered elements in two ways, by their position in the series of numbers from 1–7, or by their position in the spectrum. With the first ordering principle, we get of course:

   1, 2, 3, 4, 5, 6, 7

But with the second we get

   5, 1, 3, 2, 4, 6, 7

The ordering of the numerals by number can be thought of as the world of physical events, as in Russell's simile of the two directories, and the ordering of the numerals by their position in the spectrum can be thought of as the world of mental events.

Then we could ask the following questions.

Q: Which numeral comes after 5 in the order of numbers?

Q: Which colour comes after Y in the order of the spectrum?

These two questions have perfectly clear and unambiguous answers, '6' and 'Green'. But now consider the following apparently similar questions, which are a model for the questions behind the mind–body problem.

Q: In the sequence of numerals 1, 2, 3, 4, 5, ordered by number, which *colour* comes next? Which *colour* comes after the number 5?

Q: Which *number* comes after yellow in the spectrum?

One can ask the last two questions in a metaphysical mode. How *could* an order of colours arise from an order of numbers, when numbers are colourless? How can numbers follow colours in any order, since the two have such different properties? How can the two orders 'interact'?[24]

We can give models of the various standard solutions to the mind–body problem by answering this question for our model number elements with their colours.

Behaviourism
A colour is to be analysed in terms of the disposition of a numeral to fall into a group of numbers.

Central-state materialism
A colour is identical with a number.

Functionalism
A colour is a computational state of a number.

Eliminative materialism
A perfected science will eliminate colour descriptions in favour of the superior number descriptions.

Dualism
Colours and numbers are distinct entities.

Campbell's initial propositions can also be represented in the model of the coloured elements.

The arithmetic sequence 1–7 (= the human body) is numerical (= physical).
The spectral sequence 5–6 (= the human mind) is non-numerical (= non-physical).
The elements in the sequences 1–7 and 5–6 follow one another (= interact).
Colours and numbers do not follow one another (= interact).

This model of the mind–body problem should make us look more closely at the logical relations among the various propositions which compose it, and at the pictures which stand behind the formulation of the problems, in particular the problems of sensations and volitions.

Neutral monism is a fascinating position which is a good deal more powerful than its current neglect would lead one to expect. The crux of its solution to the mind–body problem is that it does not take the mind to be a basic entity composed of distinctively mental objects and events, or the body to be a physical entity composed of distinctively physical objects and events. To some philosophers it has seemed that the freedom which human beings have derives from the distinctively mental character of the contents of their minds, as contrasted with their bodies. For mental events are presumably insulated from external physical laws of nature. Yet this idea of a mental freedom *opposed* to the physical world does not square with neutral monism. What should a neutral monist say about the reality or unreality of human freedom?

Historical
Note

The mind–body problem, in its present form, is due to Descartes in the seventeenth century. No known solution is free of difficulties or has commanded anything approaching universal assent, though in contemporary philosophy various materialist theories are the most popular ones.

Notes

1 Keith Campbell, *Body and Mind*, Notre Dame, Ind., University of Notre Dame Press, 1984, p. 14, with the difference that I have replaced Campbell's 'spiritual' and 'spiritual thing' in his second and fourth propositions with 'non-physical' and 'non-physical thing', and 'material' and 'matter' in his first and fourth propositions with 'physical' and 'physical thing'. I shall call my four amended propositions 'Campbell's initial propositions'.

2 René Descartes, 'Meditations on First Philosophy', Meditation II, in *The Philosophical Writings of Descartes*, Vol. II, ed. and trans. John Cottingham, Robert Stoothof and Dugald Murdoch, Cambridge, Cambridge University Press, 1984.

3 Ludwig Wittgenstein, *Philosophical Investigations*, Oxford, Blackwell, 1976, Part I, Section 308.

4 Ibid., p. 100e.

5 Ibid., p. 102e.

6 J.J.C. Smart, 'Sensations and Brain Processes', *Philosophical Review* lxviii (1959), p. 147, reprinted in C.V. Borst, ed., *The Mind/Brain Identity Theory*, London, Macmillan, 1970, p. 57, Objection 1.

7 David Armstrong, *A Materialist Theory of Mind*, London, Routledge, 1968, pp. 76ff.

8 Ibid., p. 84.

9 Armstrong's response to the problem is that 'It will be seen that our formula "state of the person apt for bringing about a certain sort of behavior" is something that must be handled with care' (ibid.). All I can make of this is that care must be taken *not* to accept it! 'Perhaps it is best conceived as a slogan or catch-phrase which indicates the general lines along which accounts of the individual mental concepts are to be sought, but does no more than this.' This *seems* to mean that one should not *state* the materialist view, because of the logical circularity, but *have faith in it* anyway.

10 Hilary Putnam, *Representation and Reality*, Cambridge, Mass., MIT Press, 1988, pp. 83–84. A 'propositional attitude' is simply some psychological attitude towards a proposition, for example belief or desire. If S believes something, for example that it will rain, then, in this terminology, which is due to Bertrand Russell, S has the propositional attitude *belief*. He or she holds that the proposition 'It will rain' is true. Or if he or she desires something, for example rain, then he has the propositional attitude *desire*. S wants the proposition 'It will rain' to be true.

11 See for example Stephen Stich, *From Folk Psychology to Cognitive Science: The Case Against Belief*, Cambridge, Mass., MIT Press, 1983.

12 John W. Cook, *Wittgenstein's Metaphysics*, Cambridge, Cambridge University Press, 1994.

13 Ernst Mach, *The Analysis of Sensations and the Relation of the Physical to the Psychical*, trans. C.M. Williams, New York, Dover, 1959, p. 2.

14 Ibid.

15 Ibid., p. 9.

16 Ibid., pp. 18–19.

17 Ibid., p. 36.

18 Ibid., p. 17.

19 Ibid., pp. 18–19.

20 E.g. in Bertrand Russell, *Theory of Knowledge, the 1913 Manuscript*, ed. Elizabeth Ramsden Eames, London, Routledge, 1992, p. 12.

21 Mach, *Analysis of Sensations*, p. 12.

22 A.J. Ayer, *The Physical Basis of Mind: A Series of Broadcast Talks*, ed. Peter Laslett, Oxford, Blackwell, 1951, pp. 73–74.

23 In an earlier contribution to the talks to which Ayer's remarks were a reply, Lord Samuel had said that, 'We see, every moment, events which cannot be accounted for by derivations, however subtle, from physical and chemical processes' (ibid., p. 65).

24 The mind–body problem, on this analysis, is rather like the following riddle, which I owe to Lucy Westphal. Question: If a girl took 2.5 minutes to wash her hands, and 4.5 minutes to wash her face, what would she take to dry them? Answer: a towel.

Reading

*Brian Beakley and Peter Ludlow, eds, *The Philosophy of Mind: Classical Problems, Contemporary Issues*, Cambridge, Mass., MIT Press, 1992.

C.V. Borst, ed., *The Mind/Brain Identity Theory*, London, Macmillan, 1970.

*Keith Campbell, *Body and Mind*, Notre Dame, Ind., University of Notre Dame Press, 1984.

René Descartes, 'Meditations on First Philosophy', in *The Philosophical Writings of Descartes*, Vol. II, ed. and trans. John Cottingham, Robert Stoothoff and Dugald Murdoch, Cambridge, Cambridge University Press, 1984.

Ernst Mach, *The Analysis of Sensations and the Relation of the Physical to the Psychical*, trans. C.M. Williams, New York, Dover, 1959.

Hilary Putnam, *Representation and Reality*, Cambridge, Mass., MIT Press, 1988.

9

Freewill and Determinism
Are People Free?

A
Background

It is sometimes said that human beings are not free. They are, so the claim goes, pawns of the Fates. The Fates were three classical goddesses, Atropos, Klotho and Lachesis. Though they did not play chess, as far as we know, so that this is a mixed-up metaphor, they were the ones who decreed or said what was going to happen in human life. The English word 'fate' derives from the Latin verb *fari*, to speak, and means '"that which has been spoken, hence decreed", hence "a divine statement"'.[1] In early Greek thought, fate was personified in only one goddess, Moira, also thought to determine the course of human life. Today many people no longer believe in gods and goddesses of this sort, but we do retain a secular belief in something like 'divine statements', namely what we respectfully think of as 'laws of nature'. In the early scientific revolution, these laws of nature were conceived as reflecting the mind of God, and represented his will for the course of the world.

The dramatic claim that we are not free in our actions accordingly can locate the source of our alleged unfreedom in two very different places, depending on whether the background to the claim is theological or scientific. According to one kind of theology which denies freedom, since God is omniscient and, for good measure, omnipotent, there is no room for our freedom. If God knows that I will commit some terrible act, then it follows that I will, and I have no choice. Or so it seems.

From the scientific point of view, on the other hand, what we do, like everything else, must be capable of an explanation independent of the will of God. Our actions can be regarded, like a vector, as the sum of our inherited genes and our environment. If we are not responsible for our genes and we are not responsible for our environment, then how can we be responsible for their inevitable and calculable consequences, which are our actions?

Let us begin with this notion of scientific explanation. We need to know what it is to explain how genes plus environment add up to particular predicted actions. This raises the question what in general it means to *explain* anything.

A much-discussed model of scientific explanation, the so-called deductive-nomological model, sometimes called the 'D-N' model, makes the explanation of an event or phenomenon the *deduction* that the event occurs from a general *law* (Greek 'nomos'), plus other relevant facts.[2]

For example, why does moisture form on the outside of my jug of iced water? The explanation of this, which I shall label (3), is that:

(1)   Water vapour in air is precipitated as a liquid when it is sufficiently cooled.
(2)   The iced water in the jug sufficiently lowers the temperature of the surface and cools the air around the jug.[3]

(1) is a law, and (2) gives some particular 'initial conditions' or facts about the jug of iced water. Together, (1) and (2) imply the fact which we want explained, which is (3).

Let us consider how this model might apply to human behaviour.

Here we have:

(1)   Law
(2)   Precipitating cause or initial condition
(3)   Effect or event to be explained.

The explanation of (3) is its deduction from (1) and (2).

Let us consider how this model might – *might* – apply to human nature. Consider an imaginary city – very imaginary – in which, over a period of five years, the mean annual income (MAI) is as follows.

Year	1	2	3	4	5
MAI	$14,000	$15,000	$12,000	$7,000	$8,000

Suppose also that the number of murders (M) committed every year over the same period is also known.

Year	1	2	3	4	5
M	6	5	8	13	12

These neat numbers – *very* neat – suggest a neat law.

$$M = 20 - \frac{\text{MAI}}{1,000}$$

Imagine that we know that the MAI for the sixth year is $10,000. We then predict, on the basis of the law, that M for the sixth year is 10, by the calculation:

$$M = 20 - \frac{10,000}{1,000} = 10$$

In this calculation the precipitating cause or initial condition is the level of income, at $10,000. It should be stressed once more that these figures are fictitious, and only illustrate in a schematic way the general claim of *The Challenge of Crime in a Free Society*, the 1967 Report of the President's Commission on Law Enforcement and the Administration of Justice,[4] that 'the offender at the end of the road in prison is likely to be a member of the lowest social and economic groups in the country', itself a claim which ignores different kinds of crime (e.g. petty larceny vs. securities fraud, say, or kickbacks) and the possibility that 'the criminal justice system *selects* for arrest and imprisonment from among those who threaten society'.[5] One could also invent figures which track the relationship between *higher* income and white-collar crime. In our imaginary town, the number of white-collar crimes (WCC) is:

Year	1	2	3	4	5
WCC	28	30	24	14	16

So the law or rule is:

$$\text{WCC} = 2 \times \frac{\text{MAI}}{1,000}$$

In other words, as income goes up, so does crime – of the white-collar sort. Both the effects, murder and white-collar crime, are functions of the economic strength of our invented community. Seeing this kind of relationship, one is bound to wonder whether there is any more freedom or choice in these cases than in the case of the precipitation of water vapour. Just as temperature differences produce condensation, so changes in mean income produce, it seems, criminal actions. And if criminal human actions are determined by a law plus an initial condition, how then can they be free? It seems that we have no more freedom than a jug of iced water.

B
The Master Argument

This line of thought can be formally stated in what I will call the 'Master Argument', which includes important intermediate steps. Part of its interest is that the different views about freedom and the view that all our actions are determined, which is called 'determinism', can be generated by denying different steps in the argument. Each of these steps asserts a particular claim about the relationship between explanation, law, cause, action and freedom. The final view, known as 'hard determinism', which states that no human action is free, is generated by denying none of the steps, or by accepting them all.

	(1)	Every human action is an event.
	(2)	Every event has an explanation [*the principle of sufficient reason*].
So	(3)	Every human action has an explanation [by (1) and (2)].
But	(4)	Every explanation includes a cause [from the D-N model].
So	(5)	Every event has a cause [the *thesis of universal causation*, sometimes called *determinism*, by (2) and (4), denied by *indeterminism*].
So	(6)	Every human action has a cause [by (1) and (5)].
But	(7)	If a human action has a cause, it is not free [the *incompatibility thesis*].
And so	(8)	No human action is free [*hard determinism*, by (6) and (7), denied by *libertarianism*].

Proposition (1) means that every human action is something which takes place in the minimal sense that it can be reported in a proposition like 'This is the eleventh murder this year' or 'She took hold of her attacker and shook him just like a terrier with a rat.' An 'event' in this sense is merely something which happens.

(2) says that every proposition which reports an event can be deduced from other propositions, and that what these propositions report is the explanation of the event to be explained. These explanations include laws like 'Water vapour in air is precipitated when the air is sufficiently cooled.' If this is right, in order to deny proposition (2), we would have to imagine something which happens for absolutely no reason. This is hard. Imagine that your car won't start in the morning, but for absolutely no reason! The battery is fine, there is plenty of petrol, and everything else is working perfectly, but – for no reason! –

the car won't start.[6] Why are we *sure* that there must be something wrong, some reason at work?

(3) follows from (1) and (2).

(4) claims that every explanation includes a proposition reporting a cause. It simply unpacks the notion of an explanation given above.

(5), sometimes called the thesis of universal causation, follows from (2) and (4). The so-called 'indeterminists' deny that every event has a cause, but it is important to note that this denial does not by itself imply that human actions are free. For suppose that indeterminism is true of human action, and that no human action has a cause, but all are as random as any set of events can be. In that case I do not cause my own breathing to slow down when I wish to remain calm, but whether it slows down is a random affair. I have to wait and see whether it will. But this is hardly the affirmation of human freedom. For freedom is not the same as chance. To act freely, one would think, is to exercise some sort of control over one's actions.

Applying (5) to (1), we can infer (6).

(7) is called the incompatibility thesis because it asserts that 'has a cause' is incompatible with 'is free', in the sense that if one is true of some action, then the other is false.

Putting (6) and (7) together, we get (8), the thesis of hard determinism, which denies the existence of human freedom.

It is then a short step to a further startling conclusion, which is a moral one. If an action is not free, then responsibility cannot be ascribed to the actor. If we are all just following parts scripted for us by universal laws and precipitating causes, then we are no more responsible for these actions than actors are responsible for the actions given to the characters they are playing by the script.

C
Against Hard Determinism

The Master Argument is valid. This means that if we think that the conclusion is false, one or more of the premises must be false. Which of them is it? It is important to see that half of the steps in the argument are not premises, because they follow logically from premises. (3), (5), (6) and (8) are derivative propositions. If they are to be denied, this must be because the conjunction of the propositions from which they follow must be denied. So, for example, if we wish to deny (8), then we must deny (7) or (6) or both. The so-called *soft determinists*, who are *compatibilists*, wish to reject the incompatibility thesis. Their aim is to *reconcile* freedom and determinism. They take the view that the fact that an action is determined does not mean that it is not free. How can this be?

The answer lies in a critical distinction, which compatibilists have drawn in various ways. There is a difference, these philosophers (including the present author) will say, between two ways of what one could generically call 'being affected' by some event. On the one hand, there is simple causation. Suppose, for example, a small boy is eating his soup. We can say that he is caused to eat his soup by his hunger. On the other hand, he can be made to eat his soup, or forced to eat it, say by his mother, who is standing behind him with the soup spoon, ready to whack him if he doesn't 'Finish your nice soup.' This is more than causation. In the first case, says the compatibilist, the boy is eating freely, *because* he is not being coerced or forced. In the second case, he is not eating freely *because* he is being coerced or forced to eat.

Is it true, in the case of one of the murders committed in our model city, that the murderer was *forced* to commit it? That is, was someone standing over her and *making* her do it? If not, say those who deny the incompatibility thesis, in spite of the fact that the murderer may have been caused to do it, say by poverty and desperation, her act was free. Why? Because it proceeded from her wants, not the wants of anyone else.

There is another critical distinction which proposition (7) of the Master Argument confuses. The sets of figures for the MAI, M and WCC are descriptions of what happened, and putting them together into the laws:

$$M = 20 - \frac{MAI}{1,000} \quad \text{and} \quad WCC = 2 \times \frac{MAI}{1,000}$$

gives a relationship between these descriptions. But if the events which the descriptions describe were different, *so would the law be*. That is, the law does not *prescribe* that something happens, it merely *describes* what does happen. The law is parasitic on the descriptions. The hard determinist has confused description with prescription, and thinks that the two laws given are actually the *cause* of what happens. But they are not. They are merely descriptions of a correlation between the three sets of figures, MAI, M and WCC, and it is some sort of conceptual mistake to think that what makes someone commit a white-collar fraud is the law that the number of white-collar frauds is twice the mean income, divided by a thousand. The accused cannot offer as a justification of his or her act the proposition that he or she was only after all fulfilling his or her scientific quota, white-collar crime number 10, say, and that he or she cannot be blamed for doing his or her duty in this respect. Or rather, he or she cannot offer this defence and expect the judge to accept it!

D
The Compatibilist Analysis

Consider then an attempt at an analysis which in effect denies the incompatibility thesis, and allows correlations and causes without concluding that they force events to happen.

> S does *a* freely.
> ↓
> S does *a* and S wants to do *a*.

This analysis of freedom is perfectly consistent with saying that S was caused to do *a*. If this is right, the incompatibility thesis, which says that if S does a freely, then he or she is not caused to do it, is false.

Yet the analysis is not strong enough. Suppose that S is a boy who wants to eat his soup, but, at the same time, his mother is forcing him to eat it. What then? Does he eat it freely? By the analysis he does, because he wants to eat it. But he is also being forced to eat it. What should we say?

Compatibilists will add an extra requirement to deal with this, to the effect that S eats freely if he could have *not* eaten *if* he had not wanted to. In our example, if his mother doesn't mind whether he eats his soup or not, the little boy S could down his cutlery and refuse to eat his soup. When he is eating freely, what is true is that he could have done otherwise if he had wanted to. When he is being forced to eat, on the other hand, this is not true. 'Forced' here has a sense, I think, nearly as strong as 'force-fed', given the psychological reality of unequal power in the situation I am imagining. Even if the little boy had not wanted to, he would have had to eat his soup.

The typical compatibilist analysis is thus as follows.

> S does *a* freely.
> ↓
> S does *a*, S wants to do *a*, and S could have done otherwise if he or she had wanted.

The point of the third condition is nicely brought out in a case described by Locke. He invites us to imagine a man who is carried, while asleep, into a room, where, when he awakes, he finds himself in the company of a friend. He is happy to be in the room talking to his friend, but he does not know that the door to the room is locked.[7] He could not leave the room even if he wanted to. Are we to say that he is free, even though he is a prisoner, merely because he is enjoying the company of his friend? This would be like saying that a criminal in jail is not a prisoner merely because he is happy to be in jail, or even like saying that someone is in good health merely because she is happy to be ill. (Perhaps she welcomes the opportunity to do some reading.)

It is, however, a little hard to bend one's mind around the sentence 'S could have done otherwise if he or she had wanted' which is designed to rule out such cases. What it means is illustrated in the following diagram. On the right fork is what S wants, say to go to Salt Lake on Interstate 15. On the left, she wants to go to Idaho Falls on Interstate 15.

On the 'wants to go to SL' fork, there is a further fork. To the right, S does go to SL. To the left, she goes to IF instead, perhaps because she gets on the wrong bus. The same thing applies if she wants to go to IF. Perhaps she goes to IF, or perhaps, in spite of the fact that she wants to go to IF, for some other reason she does not. Perhaps, for example, an enormous tree has fallen across the Interstate, and all traffic is being turned back. So S wants to go to IF, but she does not go to IF. The 'branch line' which I have labelled 'goes to IF' is closed.

This is where the third condition of the compatibilist analysis comes into play. What it means to say that S could have done otherwise if she had wanted is that, if it is the case that it is true that she wants to go to IF, there is not something which prevents her from carrying out this want. And this is the heart of the analysis. The interesting thing is that whether, on the line 'wants to go to SL', S freely goes to SL does not depend on what happens on the 'wants to go to SL' line! That is, it is not the presence of some act of will that makes S go to SL which settles the question of whether she does that freely. What decides that is whether, if she had wanted to do something *else*, she could have done that something else, or whether there was something making this impossible.

Thus whether this third condition is satisfied, and whether S does a freely, does not depend on what has happened prior to her wanting to go to SL or IF. It does not matter, in particular, whether her wanting to go to SL

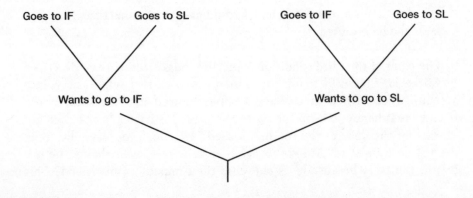

itself had strong causes. What matters is that it was *her* wish or want, according to the soft determinist.

One could add determinism to compatibilism; the resulting view is called soft determinism. It maintains that every human action is caused, but that even so, that does not interfere with their perfect freedom. Compatibilism is, so to speak, soft determinism without the determinism. Neither the presence of a cause nor the absence of a cause entitles us to infer that the action in question is freely done, or that it is not. In other words, it is open to the soft determinist to deny propositions (3) or (4) in the Master Argument, or to affirm them, and still to maintain their irrelevance to (8), hard determinism. The irrelevance here is of course due to the denial of incompatibility in (7), the incompatibility thesis.

The third condition, 'S is not forced to do a', is to be understood in both an inner and an outer sense. In the inner sense, S is not forced by, for example, a powerful compulsion which has taken over his or her mind and behaviour, or because he or she is in the grip of some overwhelming obsession. In the outer sense, it is to be understood that S is not being compelled by some superior force, or even perhaps the threat of it. When a traveller responds to the highwayman's 'Your money or your life' by handing over his wallet, this is exactly not a free act, because of the overwhelming threat to life. It seems to me to be a sophistry (a specious or tricky invalid argument with some surface plausibility) to say that the traveller makes a free choice, or hands over his wallet freely, because he chooses the highwayman's first disjunct ('your money') rather than the second ('your life'). If this were not so, then how can the highwayman have done anything wrong? All he has done is to invite the traveller to make a free choice. Can the highwayman say to the judge, in justification of his action, 'But, m'lud, it was his own *free choice* to give me his wallet. All I did was to ask . . .'? *All*?

E
Libertarianism

There is a final view we must consider, which is the view that some human actions, at least, are free, and that their freedom consists in their being brought about by uncaused acts of will. This position is known as libertarianism, for no obvious reason, as it concerns metaphysical freedom rather than political freedom, and 'liberty' is the political concept. Libertarianism in the political sense is a commitment to maximum individual liberty of action and behavior and minimal state activity within the lives of individuals. It restricts the moral authority of the state to negative functions such as policing and the enforcing of contracts. Many libertarians in this second political sense might of course also be libertarians in the metaphysical sense.

So libertarians accept that 'S does *a* freely' is sometimes true. Libertarians deny hard determinism. But they also accept the incompatibility thesis. So they are bound to deny that every human action has a cause. Which actions do not have a cause, according to them? Libertarians, in the sense that I define them, say that it is those actions which derive from the human will. Left to itself, the football will continue to travel across the goal mouth. But I inject an act of will into the causal nexus of events. I shoot, and if my eye and ball control are as good as my will, then I score. Goal! Here, according to libertarians, is an event which is to be explained by the action of the human will on the otherwise closed system of dynamical events, not by something within the system.

So in the sense in which I am using the term, 'libertarians' give the following analysis. They say that it is true that S does a freely; and:

S does *a* freely
↓
S does *a*, and *a* is produced by an act of S's will.

The trouble with this analysis is that it faces a terrible dilemma. Take S's act of will, the volition which produces the act a which is, as a result, said to be free, according to the libertarian analysis. Call this second act *a′*. Either *a′* is a free act or it is not. If it is not a free act, then it is difficult to see how or why it could generate a free act. If *a′* is a free act, on the other hand, what does this mean? The view we are examining tells us. Plugging *a′* into the libertarian analysis, we get:

S does *a′* freely.
↓
S does *a′*, and *a′* is produced by an act of S's will.

What is this 'act of S's will' in this last analysis? It cannot be *a′*, as, presumably, nothing can be the cause of itself. Well then, call it *a″*. So S does *a* freely if he does *a′*, and he does *a′* freely if he does *a″*. And then we are started on an infinite regress, in which a leads to *a′*, *a′* to *a″*, *a″* to *a‴*, *a‴* to *a⁗*, and so on. This is clearly impossible.

The conclusion to be drawn is that the original libertarian analysis is wrong. This need not surprise us, as we have already decided in favour of compatibilism. The position which results can be described as one which says that there is no freewill in the libertarian's sense, but that there is free choice in the compatibilist's sense. In the compatibilist's analysis there is no mention of either will or volitions, or of the causes which might be, or might not be, responsible for our wanting what we do want, such as hunger. We are neither hard determinist machines, nor libertarian gods, creating our actions out of nothing from inner acts of will. 'Let there be an action', says the Human Will, and there is an action. The false picture here is of the Human Will as a centre of absolute omnipotence, stronger than all the causality in the world. (This conception of freedom is sometimes known as 'contracausal' freedom.)

There is a principle, known as Ramsey's Maxim, after the English philosopher F.P. Ramsey, which states that in a conflict between two philosophical views, 'the truth lies not in one of the disputed views but in some third possibility which has not yet been thought of, which we can only discover by rejecting something assumed as obvious by both of the disputants'.[8] In this case the third proposition, which hard determinism and libertarianism agree on, is proposition (7) in the Master Argument, the incompatibility thesis. Both views agree that if an action has a cause, it cannot be free. The hard determinist believes that every human action does have a cause, and concludes that no action is free. The libertarian, on the other hand, believes that some actions are free, and concludes that they cannot have a cause. One man's *modus ponens*, as the saying goes, is another man's *modus tollens*.

Historical
Note

The question of whether human beings are or are not free, in the libertarian's sense, has been rationally discussed, with great vigour, since classical Greek times. Fear of scientific determinism has been a principal motivation for libertarianism. Another motivation for libertarianism has been its apparent harmony with religious and moral doctrine.

Notes

1 Eric Partridge, *Origins: A Short Etymological Dictionary of Modern English*, New York, Greenwich, 1983, pp. 201–202.
2 See Carl G. Hempel, *Philosophy of Natural Science*, Englewood Cliffs, N.J., Prentice Hall, 1986, p. 50, and for criticism of the D-N model, Nancy Cartwright, 'The Truth Doesn't Explain Much', *American Philosophical Quarterly* 17, 2 (1980), pp. 159–163, and also Hilary Putnam, 'The "Corroboration" of Theories', in *Mathematics, Matter and Method, Philosophical Papers*, Vol. I, Cambridge, Cambridge University Press, 1975, p. 250.

3 Ernest Nagel, *The Structure of Science: Problems in the Logic of Scientific Explanation*, Indianapolis, Ind./Cambridge, Mass., Hackett, 1979, p. 16.

4 President's Commission on Law Enforcement and the Administration of Justice, *The Challenge of Crime in a Free Society*, Washington, D.C., U.S. Government Printing Office, February 1967.

5 Jeffrey Reiman, *The Rich Get Richer and the Poor Get Poorer*, New York, Macmillan, 1990, p. 117.

6 James W. Cornman, Keith Lehrer and George S. Pappas, *Philosophical Problems and Arguments*, Indianapolis, Ind./Cambridge, Mass., Hackett, 1992, p. 92.

7 John Locke, *An Essay Concerning Human Understanding*, ed. Peter H. Nidditch, Oxford, Oxford University Press, 1975, Book II, Ch. XXI, p. 238.

8 F.P. Ramsey, 'Universals', in *Philosophical Papers*, ed. Hugh Mellor, Cambridge, Cambridge University Press, 1990, pp. 11–12.

Reading

D.F. Pears, ed., *Freedom and the Will*, London, Macmillan, 1963.

Gilbert Ryle, 'Introduction to Philosophy: The Freedom of the Will', in *Aspects of Mind*, ed. René Meyer, Oxford, Blackwell, 1993.

Michael Slote, 'Understanding Free Will', *Journal of Philosophy* 77, No. 3 (1980), pp. 138–151.

Michael Thorp, *Free Will*, London, Routledge and Kegan Paul, 1981.

Gary Watson, ed., *Free Will*, Oxford, Oxford University Press, 1982.

David Wiggins, 'Towards a Reasonable Libertarianism', in his *Needs, Values, Truth*, Oxford, Blackwell, 1991.

10
The Meaning of Life
What Is the Meaning of Life?

A
Aristotle's Problem

To many the question 'What is the meaning of life?' seems to be a nebulous one, unanswerable and therefore not worth asking. There is also a less common but related reaction, that the question is nebulous and unanswerable, and *therefore* worth pondering. Between these two reactions, the cynical and the obscurantist, lies, I think, the truth. The question is of enormous practical and personal importance, and so it is worth trying to get clear about it. It ought to be possible to do so, because there could be after all no reason why *this* question should be necessarily less clear than any other.

As a preliminary, let us consider the *oddity* of the words in which we express our question. I believe that our modern formulation of the question is a secular or post-theistic version of an essentially theistic formulation. In Christian theology, for example, one encounters the concept of *eternal life*. Eternal life in God is the final destination of human life. So when modern science put the Christian theological cosmology in question, by producing evidence of infinite and empty time and space, those who lost their faith as a result were bound to ask, since eternity is not the meaning of life, 'What – what *then* – is the meaning of life?'[1] They were not distressed by the fact and size of infinite space and time. Those might have represented joy and freedom, as to an explorer, rather than a heavy burden. Or there might have been rejoicing in the discovery of our humble position in the universe. ('We are but worms.') What was distressing was not the objective size of the universe, but rather the sudden and vertiginous *difference* between the size it had seemed to be and the size it actually was, the sudden *transition* from the cosy medieval cosmos to the larger scientific one.[2] Our modern Western version of the question of the meaning of life is given in the shadow of the rejection of the Christian answer and of the structure and character of the Christian answer itself.

Quite apart from the historical overlay which the question now carries, though, it must also have a clear sense, or we will be justified in taking the usual line of least resistance, dismissing it with mild curiosity, humour and otherwise lack of interest. It is sometimes said that everyone must determine the meaning of life for herself or himself. What this brutalist evasion[3] of the question misses is that the *question* still has to be answered of *what* it is that everyone is being enjoined to determine for himself or herself. Q: 'I don't understand the question.' A: 'Just answer the question, please.' Or compare the difficult and important question 'How should I vote?' with the evasive and pseudo-democratic answer 'Everyone must vote for herself or himself', which is no help at all and which everybody already knows.

I want to begin discussion of the meaning of life at a slight distance from the problem, with an ethical issue which has a very similar logical structure. The point of this exercise is to see how much of the problem of the meaning of life is derived from a logic which it shares with other problems, such as the foundation of ethics and value, and the question of what the *summum bonum* or best good is.

Consider Aristotle's clear-headed exposition, at the beginning of the *Nichomachean Ethics*,[4] of the central logical puzzle which one runs into with this last question. Aristotle begins with the observation that every action 'is aimed at some good'.[5] This good is the 'end' of the action, or the point of it, as we could say. There are *many* such points or ends, however. Aristotle's examples are health, which is the end of medicine, a boat, which is the end of boatbuilding, and victory, which is the end of generalship. (Military officers today would be more circumspect, perhaps, and would identify peace as their end, although they would also perhaps be ready to concede that this peace is achieved by victory in warfare.) Some ends are also 'subordinate' to other ends, however, such as bridlemaking to horse riding. In such a case, Aristotle thinks, the superordinate activity is 'more choiceworthy', a *better* good, than the subordinate one. So he gives us a picture of an ascending hierarchy of actions or activities, the good getting better as the hierarchy ascends. The picture raises a crucial puzzle.

The Means-Only Puzzle
Since we choose everything we do for a further end, unless there is a supreme end or best good, 'it will go on without limit, making desire empty and futile'.[6] If everything we do is a means to an end and not itself the ultimate end, and if the point of doing anything is its end, then nothing in life will have any point.

By the 'it' which 'will go on without limit' in the passage quoted in the means-only puzzle, Aristotle means the process of one action being given its point by another action which is its superior.

Thus, for example, we study in order to learn. We wish to learn in order to pass exams. We wish to pass exams in order to get a good degree. We wish to get a good degree so as to get a good job. We wish to get a good job because of the pay. We wish to get paid well so that we can buy the things we want. We wish to buy the things we want in order to . . . And so on. Where and what is the end to this apparently endless road? Wherever and whatever it is, Aristotle says, the following two conditions will determine its existence.

1   The best good is *complete*, in the sense that it is chosen for itself alone and not for a yet further end.

2   The best good is *self-sufficient*, in the sense that all 'by itself it makes a life choiceworthy and lacking nothing'.[7]

Aristotle adds three riders to these conditions. For condition 1, he makes the distinction between an end which is complete and one which is unconditionally complete or complete 'without qualification'. By this he means an end which is *never* chosen or pursued because of something else. A miser, for example, might consider that money is the best good, and that it satisfies the completeness condition 1, because 'it is chosen for itself and not for a further end.' Yet misers would not count money as *unconditionally* complete, because they know that sometimes they have to spend it in order to get something else. So Aristotle insists that the best good of condition 1 must be unconditionally complete as well as complete.

Of the self-sufficiency condition 2, Aristotle notes that it does not mean what is adequate for the life of a hermit or a solitary person, 'but what suffices also for parents, children, wife and in general for friends and fellow-citizens, since a human being is a naturally political [animal]'. He adds with characteristic common sense that, 'Here however, we must impose some limit, for if we extend the good to parents' parents and childrens' children and to friends of friends, we shall go on without limit.'[8] Aristotle also remarks of condition 2 that the unit for which the best good is sufficient is 'a complete life. For one swallow does not make a spring, nor does one day; nor, similarly, does one day or a short time make us blessed and happy.'[9]

There is only one thing which can satisfy these conditions and qualifications, Aristotle says, and that is *happiness* or human flourishing. We always choose happiness for its own sake, because of itself, and never as a means to an end. Though this cannot be true without exception, it is easy to see that it is mostly true. (An exception would be someone who knows that she or he must be happy in order to solve a certain problem, and deliberately sets out to make herself or himself happy *in order to* be able to solve that problem.) Happiness is also self-sufficient, because after all the person who has chosen a happy life has chosen a life with which he or she is *happy*!

The following analysis is the first step in Aristotle's argument. 'Every craft and every investigation, and likewise every action and decision, seems to aim at some good.'[10] This says:

> S does *a*.
> ↓
> S does *a* because *r*.

We could call this the thesis of instrumental rationality (*a* is the instrument, and 'because' makes *r* a reason (Latin *ratio*) for doing it). All human action is rational, so the analysis claims, in the sense that it is done for some end which supplies the reason for the action. In the analysis *a* is the craft, investigation, act or decision, and *r* is its good. The end, point or meaning of *a* is then *r*. But every end *r* is itself something which must have meaning or point. Hence

> ↓
> S does *a* because *r*, and *r* because *s*, and *s* because *t*, and *t* because *u* . . .

and we have the means-only puzzle.

Yet if anything is to have an end whose value does not leak out into the next *s*, and then *t*, and then *u* and then finally down the drain of the three little dots, making 'desire empty and futile', there must be a final end or dot which stops the 'value leakage'.

> ↓
> S does *a* because *r*, and *r* because *s*, and *s* because *t*, and *t* because *u* . . . because E.

E will be the best good, the final end, which must according to Aristotle satisfy conditions 1 and 2 and which he identifies with happiness, H.

> ↓
> S does *a* because *r*, and *r* because *s*, and *s* because *t*, and *t* because *u* . . . because E, and E is H.

The problem of the meaning of life can be formulated with exactly the same logical structure. In this formulation the problem is that if the meaning of *a* is *r*, *r* must itself have meaning. Let the meaning of *r* be *s*. Then in order for *r* to have meaning, *s* must have meaning. Since in order for *a* to have meaning, *r* must have meaning, in order for *a* to have meaning, *s* must have meaning.

Aristotle's analysis has three steps.

1   The addition of 'because *r*', with the resulting regress to *u* and on.
2   The deduction of a single final end E, to halt the regress.
3   The identification of E with happiness, on the basis of conditions 1 and 2.

There are difficulties with each step.

1(a)   Some things are not done for a reason, purpose or end. Not all reading, for example, is ultimately done for the sake of happiness or, exactly, of anything else. If the answer to 'Why are you reading that book about the structure of politics at the accession of George III?' was 'Because it makes me happy', one would suspect either dilettantism or a very deep interest in English history. The more neutral answer, 'Because I want to', sounds petulant, like a response to a suggestion that doing something other than reading that particular book was a good idea, such as washing the dishes. Again, if the answer was, 'To promote human flourishing or happiness' (*eudaimonia* is the transliteration of the Greek word), one would suspect insincerity or pretension, or a far better grasp of the relationship between private and individual actions and the collective good than is warranted by any available evidential connections. In general neither individual or collective 'happiness' nor 'wanting to' is the usual true answer to the question of why one is reading the book.

But nor is it correct to say that one had no end or no end in mind, *if* this was taken to mean that one was reading the book for no *reason*. That would sound as if one had picked up the book idly, or for want of something better to do, and was just flipping through it. I do not believe that it is known why *in general* people read books, or that there must be any one answer. There is surely a host of different reasons, ranging from pleasure to acquiring information, and other indescribable ones, but there must be just as many ways in which people read a book, not for no reason, in the sense of no reason at all, but merely *not* for any specified reason.

It is interesting to see an extreme and misstated version of this point of view in Moritz Schlick's 'On the Meaning of Life'.[11] It is misstated because it accepts a proposition which performs the same role as the thesis of instrumental rationality. Schlick locates the meaning of life in actions which are done for *no* purpose.

The core and ultimate value of life can only lie in such states as

exist for their own sake and carry their satisfaction in themselves ... If such activities exist, then in them the seemingly
divided is reconciled, means and end, action and consequence
are fused into one, we have then found ends-in-themselves
which are more than end-points of acting and resting-points of
existence, and it is these alone that can take over the role of the
true content of life. There really are such activities. To be
consistent, we must call them *play*, since that is the name for
free, purposeless action, that is, action which in fact carries its
purpose within itself.[12]

Schlick distinguishes between purpose and meaning, and argues that
'we shall never find an ultimate meaning in existence, if we view it only
under the aspect of purpose',[13] including presumably the purpose of happiness or human flourishing. He accepts a version of the thesis of instrumental rationality, the first crucial step in the logic behind Aristotle's
version of the means-only puzzle, and the regress it generates. He
attempts to stop the regress by finding termini in which the distinction
between means and ends has no application, not realizing that in adopting
this solution he has accepted the very thesis which he wishes to deny.
Schlick *accepts* the proposition that the purpose of any activity derives
from something else, and infers that there must be activities of ultimate
worth without purpose. The worth of these activities must then not
depend on the worth of any others.

In the *Summa Contra Gentiles* St Thomas Aquinas makes an interesting criticism of a point of view like Schlick's,[14] but he too accepts the logic
of the problem, for he solves it by identifying E, the final end of life, with
happiness, H, and further identifying H with something he calls 'ultimate'
happiness, and this in turn with 'the contemplation of the truth', which for
him is God. His reasoning is completely in line with the structure of
Aristotle's problem. The contemplation of God answers Aristotle's condition 1, unconditional completeness, because, St Thomas argues, the contemplation of truth 'is not directed to anything further as to its end, since
the contemplation of truth is sought for its own sake'. It must uniquely
satisfy Aristotle's condition 2, self-sufficiency, because 'this operation
alone is proper to man',[15] and so for him there is nothing else which could
make a life choiceworthy by itself. St Thomas claims for his own choice of
highest good the virtue of supreme *stability*. It is natural, he says, 'to
desire unfailing endurance in one's goods', and only God, being perfect,
can provide it.[16]

1(b)   There is another problem with the thesis of instrumental rationality, which is a critical ambiguity. Suppose a case in which it is true to say
that *r* is the reason for *a*, or that '*a* because *r*'. This could mean either that

as a matter of fact S is doing a for r, for example S is growing an ugly hedge to spite his neighbours. This really is S's reason (our long-suffering S has turned nasty at last!), but (and here is the ambiguity) we could say to him, of the irritation he has felt towards his neighbours, which has built up over the years and has at last turned into spite, that *that* is no reason for growing an ugly and expensive hedge. So it is the reason, but it is no reason!

There are obviously two senses of 'reason' here. In the second sense, which means roughly 'justification' or '*good* reason', many actions do not have a reason at all, and the thesis of instrumental rationality is *false*. There is no compelling reason, no good reason, indeed no reason at all for me to sit in the garden this afternoon. All sorts of vaguely plausible but untrue reason could be invented. St Thomas' 'that the mind may be relaxed, and that thereby we may afterwards become more fit for studious occupations' belongs to this class of regimentalizing distortions of the facts of motivation to fit the thesis of instrumental rationality. In the sense of lacking a justification or reason, many actions are quite free, and for this reason are better termed 'activities'. Compare 'his actions on the morning of the 25th' with 'his activities on the morning of the 25th', which sounds more bumbling and undirected – freer.

2   In addition, Aristotle takes an amazing misstep at the outset. He says that everything aims at some good, and deduces from this that there must be some *single* good, at which everything aims. This is absurd. The fact that there is some target at which every arrow is directed does not mean that every arrow is directed at the *same* target. Aristotle has confused 'Every arrow has some target', not necessarily the same one, with 'There is one target, and that one target is the target every arrow has.'

3   The relevance of the discussions of Schlick and St Thomas, given above under 1(a) and 1(b) suggests that it is not the case that only happiness can block the regress by satisfying the unconditional completeness condition. Of course this will be the case if happiness is defined as Schlick defines play, as anything in which the action which is the means and the state which is the end are combined. But this would have little to recommend it as a definition of happiness except that it allows Aristotle his conclusion that E and H are identical.

These doubts suggest in one way or another that Aristotle's solution to the means-only puzzle is too schematic. This is inevitable given the thesis of instrumental rationality, and the picture of human action which feeds it. Here is the action, there is the end which it achieves. The same diagnosis – overschematization – is even easier to make of Albert Camus' discussion of the problem of the meaning of life, the most passionately argued and celebrated in modern literature. It has considerably more rhetorical fire than Aristotle's account of the logic of the best good, though also correspondingly less logical organization. Surprisingly, it too depends on the thesis of instrumental rationality.

B
Camus' Formulation

Camus is such a great literary stylist that his views are difficult to summarize without misrepresentation. It is therefore hard to criticize them, or to disagree with them. But it is possible.

> All great deeds and all great thoughts have a ridiculous beginning. Great works are often born on a streetcorner or in a restaurant's revolving door. So it is with absurdity. The absurd world more than others derives its nobility from its abject birth. In certain situations replying 'nothing' when asked what one is thinking about may be pretense in a man. Those who are loved are well aware of this. But if the reply is sincere, if it symbolizes that odd state of soul in which the void becomes eloquent, in which the chain of daily gestures is broken, in which the heart seeks the link that will connect it again, then it is as it were the first signs of absurdity.
>
> It happens that the stage sets collapse. Rising, streetcar, four hours in the office or the factory, meal, streetcar, four hours of work, meal, sleep, and Monday Tuesday Wednesday Thursday Friday and Saturday according to the same rhythm – this path is easily followed most of the time. But one day the 'why' arises and everything begins in that weariness tinged with amazement.[17]

The second paragraph is an argument for absurdity. 'It happens that the stage sets collapse.' That is, we become aware of the ultimate meaninglessness or absurdity of life. Aristotle's question 'Why?' arises. Why get out of bed now? To catch the tram. Why catch the tram? To get to the office or factory. Why go there? To work. For what? To earn money. Why earn money? To eat a meal. And so on. Camus' description is a marvellous evocation of a human existence which resembles nothing so much as a hamster on a wheel. The only reason the hamster does not find its life on the wheel meaningless is because it doesn't know that it is not going anywhere. If it did, it would, like us, feel 'that weariness tinged with amazement'.

Looked at a little more closely and less poetically, though, differences between our lives and those of the hamster start to appear. Let us study Camus' man, the absurd man who rises, catches the tram, and finally returns, to sleep. Let us call this man AM, for 'Absurd Man', or perhaps for 'AM Man', the man of the deserted early morning and of the void, and let us look in detail at the routine which defines him.

1 'Rising'. Camus does not refer to AM by name or description, but only with the gerund of AM's activities: 'rising'. 'There is rising.' The implied passivity gives a drugged or mechanical feel to the description of AM getting out of bed, and he already sounds a little tired. Already the wheel of the hamster seems to turn. AM does not jump, or slither or crawl out of bed. He 'rises'. What then? He has no breakfast, no coffee, no orange juice, not even a little croissant. He does not greet his wife, if AM is a man, or her husband, if AM is a woman. (If 'Absurd Woman' sounds a little absurd, that is because on the whole, until now, the lives of women have been less directly under the spell of market forces and the thesis of instrumental rationality or distant goal-seeking.) In fact there is nothing to say which sex AM is.

At any rate he (supposing AM to be a man) is single, lacking a Significant Other, SO, because his life is absurd or minus significance, and also childless. He is not – not he – forced out of bed by the pounding of little feet, and the shrill demands of legions of children to get up and dismantle the chimney of the wood-stove instantly and release the bird trapped in it. For him, it is 'rising', with a languid French elegance.

In spite of his classless nature (for he is also MM, Minimal Man), one cannot avoid seeing AM, on 'rising', sliding into nothing but a silk dressing-gown. He has few possessions, but, perhaps, they are not inelegant. He does not brush his teeth, or wonder about his thinning hair, or whether the drain in the bathroom needs unclogging, and how he is going to do this without losing his temper with his wife, with whom he has pleaded not to wash her hair in the sink. AM's morning so far is quite painless. He has not even forgotten to feed the dog, because there is no dog.

2 'Streetcar'. Detached and silent, yet strong, AM glides out of his house (tent? adobe hut? shack? cave? semi-detached? skyscraper?), to the tram. He is alone, aloof even, and there is no mention of the pointless but nice little conversations and contretemps which typically make people late for their morning ride, or even miss it altogether. Once on the tram, there is no sound, or none described, no clanking or shrieking of the rails, no regular seat, warm from the previous passenger, no newspaper to read, and no passing scene to watch, and no romantic 'glance', or even a smile, at a fellow passenger. Just – 'streetcar'.

3   'Four hours in the office or the factory'. We know that AM does not work on a farm or in a hospital, or as a labourer or an artist. He is an urban creature, and he works an eight-hour day, exactly four hours before noon and four hours after.

4   'Meal'. At last AM stops and eats, but Camus does not tell us what. We are also not told where, whether he has a brown-bag lunch at the factory bench, or goes, from the office, to a restaurant, with a revolving door. But either way, after lunch he does something very odd. He takes to the tram again.

5   'Streetcar'. Where does he go? Wherever it is, he ends up back at work (6), so perhaps he goes for an innocent 'circular' tour. Or perhaps he is *returning* to work from the restaurant with the revolving door, having had too much wine. In that case he walked *to* the restaurant, and he did not have a brown-bag lunch. Or perhaps he was visiting someone . . . But then how did he get back to the office or factory? The sequence is evidently confused, but one thing is clear; the next thing is work.

6   'Four hours of work'. AM works an exact number of hours in the p.m., four, just as in the a.m. We know that he works in an office or factory, and so he is probably not self-employed, and his work is also not work with variable hours, such as surgery or sculpture. In other words, his work is interesting and important to him, and to Camus, only in exactly the same way as his other mechanical actions (rising, streetcar, meal, sleep), as means to an end. One suspects indeed that his work is experienced not as meaningful or interesting but as a kind of *somnambulance*. Indeed, there is a convincing interpretation of Camus which says that he was really concerned to describe not the metaphysically alienated condition of humankind as a whole, but the economically and mentally alienated conditions of the Algerians among whom he lived and worked before he came to France, also described in his great novels.

7   'Meal'. Not 'dinner', which sounds interesting, but 'meal' – again – a solitary and cheerless affair, just bread like the brown-bag lunch, without joy, or conversation, or wine (certainly not after the unfortunate mix-up with the tram at lunch-time). AM does not look out of the window, he has no coffee after dinner, there is no time allotted for recreation, or hobbies, or walking along the river with a friend, or talking over the fence to a neighbour. No, AM, completely isolated, as far as one can tell, goes straight to sleep at the table.

8   'Sleep'. And there it ends. His life is complete and self-sufficient,

disturbed not even by a wrong telephone number during the night, or a barking dog, or a confused call from his aunt in Rouen. He has had not one human encounter during the day, and his sleep is merely a preparation for the next mechanical round of activities.

9   AM's week. AM follows the same cycle of six minimal activities six days a week, including Saturday. He works on Saturday. It is interesting that Camus does not use punctuation in his litany of the days of the week, giving the effect of an empty calendar: MON. TUES. WED. and so on. For nothing at all happens in AM's life! Camus also seems to be troubled by the fact that the days of the week keep rotating in an endless cycle. 'Not Thursday again, Thursday *always* comes after Wednesday, I can't stand it, it's so *depressing*.' But how could it be otherwise? Would it help if the calendar were rearranged so that the names of the days of the week were distributed *randomly* each week? Clearly not, and Camus' complaint is seen for what it is, a confusion between the abstract and empty description of the structure of the week, and the *contents* of the week. And Camus simply leaves out what is for many the best and most fulfilling day of the week, Sunday, which does not appear at all on AM's calendar. For Sunday is the day of rest, and AM does not rest. (He sleeps.) He is not refreshed, he does not put on a clean shirt, he does not worship his God, either in a church, or by reading the Sunday paper and playing with the dog and contemplating the foolishness of all those other benighted idiots who waste their time in church. AM worships AM, not the I AM.

In short, AM is not human. He has being of a sort, but he has no life. The extraordinary thing about him is that we are supposed to recognize ourselves in his bleak situation. We are supposed to abstract away from the real content of life, of friends, family, problems, pets, the happiness, interest and pain of daily work. And then, having removed everything that gives life interest and point from the picture, including the opportunity of a life of faith on the missing Sunday, that is, having described life minus anything which matters, and reduced it to an abstract schema, Camus solemnly declares that it is all absurd and without point, and that nothing matters. But of course there is no point to it, as *he* has described it! The problem is not the metaphysical organization of life, or lack of it, but Camus' own description of it. The rewards of life are not in its abstract structure, or in its ultimate goal, but in what it brings daily. What is also amazing about Camus' picture is that it includes no really difficult problems of life. AM has no handicapped brother, for example, about whom he is worried and concerned, but whom he also finds very difficult and embarrassing. Nor does AM experience the kinds of thing that happen in life when his brother starts to improve and his life starts to work out. AM shows no sign of being in trouble at any level, and this is part of his dimensionless and meaningless character. There is nothing that AM can *succeed* at or overcome, and that is why he can never feel entitled to genuine rest, and his life is pointless and without end.

Camus is, rather surprisingly, at one with Aristotle. Both of them believe in some version of the thesis of instrumental rationality, that everything is done *for* something else. They both believe that *if* the value of what we do does not terminate in some ultimate value, what we do has no value at all. The difference between them is that Camus thinks that our actions do *not* serve some giant and ultimate end, and tries to prove it with his description of a life lived without ends, whereas Aristotle thinks that our actions are *not* meaningless, and that therefore they *do* serve some ultimate end, namely happiness. Here again, 'one man's *modus ponens* is another man's *modus tollens.*' But both philosophers are mistaken, because the thesis of instrumental rationality is false.

C
'Nothing Matters'

In an essay called 'Nothing Matters', whose title is a reference to a sentence in Camus' novel *L'Etranger*, Richard Hare describes how a young Swiss guest in his house in Oxford came, as a result of reading Camus' novel, actually to *believe* that nothing matters. The boy was seriously affected by his new belief, in spite of the fact that up until that point, 'he was about as well-balanced a young man as you could find. There was, however, no doubt at all about the violence with which he had been affected by what he read.'[18] Hare's response was to try to help the boy to understand what it means to say that something matters or that it is important. He got the boy to agree that to say that something matters is to say that it matters *to* someone. For example,

> My wife matters.
> ↓
> My wife matters to me.

This in turn means that

> ↓
> I care about my wife.

What had gone wrong in the young man's thinking was that he had not appreciated that this last proposition reveals the real form of 'My wife matters.' He was led astray by the apparent logical form of this proposition, which is 'The subject S, my wife, has the property, or predicate, *mattering*.' That is, the form of the original proposition seems to be the same as:

> My wife chatters to me.

One can see immediately that 'My wife matters to me' and 'My wife chatters to me' do *not* have the same logical form by putting them in the passive voice. Then we would get for the second: 'I am chattered to by my wife', and for the first 'I am mattered to by my wife.' But this last sentence is complete nonsense. Mattering is not something that my wife does to me. Nor, by the way, is it something *I* do to her.

In the proposition about my wife chattering the subject is 'my wife', and 'chatters to me' is a predicate in good standing. If one thought that 'mattering' was a predicate like 'chattering', one might wonder what this activity is, called mattering. One might then 'begin to observe the world closely (aided perhaps by the clear cold descriptions of a novel like that of Camus) to see if one can catch anything doing something that could be called mattering'.[19] Failing to detect it, like a fluorescent blue-green glow, one might then *agree* with Camus. Or one might conclude that mattering is unobservable *because* it is metaphysical, and therefore invisible except to the trained literary eye. These two positions are not very far apart.

The question for Hare's friend then was what it comes to to say that X matters.

> X matters.
> ↓
> S cares about X.

So 'X does not matter' means that it is not the case that S cares about X.

Now the question is, *who* is this somebody S who does not care about anything? Hare suggests three possibilities.

1 S is Camus, the author of *L'Etranger*.
2 S is Meursault, the character in *L'Etranger* who utters the words.
3 S is the reader of *L'Etranger*, Hare's young friend.

The first possibility, Hare says, can be dismissed, because Camus obviously cared about many things. 'For to produce a work of art as good as this novel is something which cannot be done by someone who is not most

deeply concerned, not only with the form of the work, but with its content.'[20] Meursault, by the end of Camus' novel, when 'something inside
me snapped' and he grabs the priest's collar and yells at him that 'Nothing,
nothing matters',[21] evidently cares with inarticulate passion about *something*, even if only his own views. 'There is something of a contradiction in
being so violently concerned to express unconcern; if nothing *really* mattered to him, one feels, he would have been too bored to make this rather
dramatic scene', Hare comments.[22] Finally, what about Hare's young
friend?

> I therefore asked him whether it was really true that nothing
> mattered to him. And of course it was not true. He was not in
> the position of the prisoner, but in the position of most of us; he
> was concerned not about nothing, but about many things. His
> problem was not to find something to be concerned about –
> something that mattered – but to reduce to some sort of order
> those things which were matters of concern to him; to decide
> which mattered most; which he thought worth pursuing even at
> the expense of some of the others – in short, to decide what he
> really wanted.[23]

D
A Final Problem

So far Hare's analysis is illuminating, provided that one bears in mind that
mattering, having an *end*, having a *point*, and having a *meaning* are all
very different notions which raise very different problems of analysis.

Even so, there is a question which remains, and which I can best express
as follows. If mattering is just (just!) a matter of someone feeling concern,
isn't it then just *subjective*? Whether my wife matters to me then becomes
just like the question of whether it matters to me whether I have sorbet or
summer pudding for dessert. I could say, 'It doesn't matter' or 'I don't
mind', and this would be an expression of 'unconcern' in Hare's sense. Or,
if it does matter to me, I will reject the sorbet, say, and choose the summer
pudding. But none of this is a matter, really, of mattering in the important
sense in which the claim that 'Nothing matters' is supposed to be true.
Accordingly, 'I care about my wife' cannot be the correct analysis of 'My
wife matters.'

One might then try to interpret 'X matters', *ethically*, as 'I *ought* to
care about X', or *theologically*, as 'God cares about X.' These interesting
analyses would have the advantage of not allowing it to be false that my
wife ceases to matter if I die before her, and there is no one left to care for

her. For she still matters, and not just in the hypothetical sense that I would care for her if I were not dead, or in the sense that I will actually go on caring for her from beyond the grave. This means that mattering is also an objective affair. 'X matters' does not become false when whomever X matters to ceases to care about X. How can this 'objectivist' fact be expressed consistently with Hare's analysis?

Part of the answer is that what could be called the objectivity of mattering is not entirely missing from Hare's analysis, but one must look for it in the right place. This place is located by the question of what the differences are between the *ways* in which summer pudding matters to me, and the ways in which my wife matters to me.

There are several.

First: I don't matter to the summer pudding and it is not aware of my presence. The sense in which I care about my wife is altered by the fact that she is a sentient being, and by the fact that she could also care about me, even if she doesn't. If she does, of course, this will add an extra dimension to my caring about her.

Second: even though it does matter to me whether I get the sorbet or the summer pudding, if I am well mannered, that fact itself does not much matter (except to my host or hostess). 'It *shouldn't* matter' is perhaps the right way to express the point. That is, the summer pudding matters a lot on the scale from nothing through sorbet to summer pudding, but the scale itself, or rather what it scales – which pudding to choose from the ones on offer – does not matter very much. Which wife to have matters very much.

Third: it also matters in a qualitatively completely different way. One could not imagine the following words, under any circumstances, being appropriate for the choice of pudding. The celebration and blessing of a marriage in *The Book of Common Prayer* declares, 'Therefore marriage is not to be entered into unadvisedly or lightly, but reverently, deliberately, and in accordance with the purposes for which it was instituted by God.' Some of the premises for this conclusion are theological. Others are not, for example that 'The union of husband and wife in heart, body and mind is . . . for the help and comfort given one another in prosperity and adversity.' Then comes the solemn 'therefore': 'Therefore marriage is not to be entered into unadvisedly or lightly.' The point is that quite apart from the theology, the relationship of a man to his pudding is or should be utterly and completely different from the relationship of a man to his wife or hers to him.

It is not those who subscribe to Hare's analysis who do not see these differences, but those who reject his analysis on the grounds of subjectivity and superficiality. They reject the analysis because they cannot see the difference between different kinds and degrees of care and concern. For these people all kinds and degrees of care are lumped together as 'subject-ive'. Nevertheless, they do have a good question. Is it really true that there is no concept of mattering which is not mattering *to* some subject S?

Suppose it is said that social class doesn't matter. Is this supposed to mean that there is someone for whom it doesn't matter? Rather, surely, it means that even if in a subjective sense it does matter to everyone, in some further sense it does not after all matter, and should not matter. What is this further sense?

One part of it is the contribution which the thing in question makes to some larger whole. In this case this larger context is the lives of individuals and society as a whole. It is a simple truth, if it is a truth, that society would be better off without social classes, certainly of the kind which existed, say, in Victorian Britain. This is one kind of mattering. It too is a 'mattering *to*', but what something matters to is not only a person but could also be any sort of larger enterprise. Engine oil, for example, matters to the running of an engine, but not because the engine makes a conscious positive value-judgement about the oil.

It will, of course, be immediately said that this kind of mattering is dependent on whether the larger whole *itself* matters. Does the running of the engine matter? This question, I think, is mistaken, because whether or not the smooth running of the engine matters in any wider context, or matters to any person, it remains true that it would not happen without the engine oil. In this sense of mattering, mattering is insulated from the wider contexts.

There is another and related kind of mattering which is important in trying to get a fix on mattering in any objective sense.

A preliminary warning needs to be made. The *Oxford English Diction-ary (OED)* notes that the verb 'to matter' usually appears in negative and interrogative contexts. (Perhaps it retains some of the sense of the noun from which it is derived, as used in the sentence, 'Oh dear, what can the matter be?' This is the idea, as the *OED* has it, of the circumstance or state of things concerning a person or thing, especially one calling for explan-ation or remedy.) The negative use is important partly because it seems to confirm Hare's analysis. It is also significant because if the negative and interrogative uses of the notion are primary, and the centre of gravity of the concept is with 'It *doesn't* matter' and '*Does* it matter?', this gives a reason to expect, what is the case, that the positive and objective 'matter-ing' will seem to evaporate on inspection.

Consider any activity which matters in the sense that it makes a differ-ence to whether or not or how well something else takes place. Good roads matter to travel. Without them, there is no travel, or anyway worse travel. So roads matter to travel and contribute to it. But there is a relationship in the opposite direction which is less obvious but equally important. If roads matter to travel because they contribute to it, then equally the institution of travel and transport is responsible for the existence of roads. Roads get their 'mattering' from 'riding' and 'raiding' and travelling generally, as well as contributing to it. The 'smaller' thing, here roads, contributes to the larger and gets its importance this way, but the larger thing, here travel and transport, also contributes to the smaller, and it *gives* importance to them as well as getting it from them.

And of course, for theistic religious believers, allegedly 'subjective' mattering in Hare's sense does *not* exclude what for them is the most important kind of mattering, namely God's care. In Robert Bolt's play *A Man for All Seasons*, the ambitious Richard Rich, wanting to become a grandee, asks his friend Sir Thomas More who would know it, if he merely became a fine teacher. Sir Thomas' answer is, 'You, your pupils, your friends, God. Not a bad public, that . . .'.[24] A relationship of marriage or a commitment to work is deepened and strengthened and given even more meaning by what the believer believes is its theological context, which is God's 'care' or love for the whole world, whereas a relationship to a pudding is not, or anyway much less.

Historical Note

The big biblical formulation of the question of the meaning of life comes in Ecclesiastes.

> What profit has a man for all his labor / In which he toils under the sun? / One generation passes away, and another generation comes. But the earth abides forever[25] . . . / Therefore I hated life because the work that was done under the sun was distressing to me, for all is vanity and grasping at the wind[26]

as well as the biblical answer:

> I have seen the God-given task with which the sons of men are to be occupied. / He has made everything beautiful in its time. Also he has put eternity in their hearts, except that no one can find out the work that God does from beginning to end. / I know that nothing is better for them than to rejoice, and to do good in their lives.[27]

Aristotle's theory of human flourishing was married to the medieval Christian view of the contemplation of God as the greatest good by St

Thomas Aquinas. Materialist philosophers have tended, against the theists, to say that life is meaningless, but that we must make the best of it. Contemporary analytic philosophers have tried to get clearer about the possible sense of the question itself, whereas the existentialist philosophers have wanted to look for some attitude towards life – any attitude – which will keep absurdity at bay.

Notes

1 According to Wittgenstein, what they had misunderstood was the concept of eternal life. 'If we take eternity to mean not infinite temporal duration but timelessness, then eternal life belongs to those who live in the present.' Ludwig Wittgenstein, *Tractatus Logico-Philosophicus*, trans. D.F. Pears and B.F. McGuinness, London, Routledge, 1961, 6.4311, p. 72.

2 It is this historical and cultural fact, and not, as Thomas Nagel claims (in 'The Absurd', in his *Mortal Questions*, Cambridge, Cambridge University Press, 1979) the metaphysics of the structure of reflective self-consciousness, which explains why the images of the vastness of the universe have provided the 'natural expression for the sense' that life is absurd.

3 'Brutalist' because it allows only room for determination and *decision*, or power, and not for truth and *discovery*.

4 Aristotle, *Nichomachean Ethics*, trans. Terence Irwin and Gail Fine, in *Aristotle Selections*, Indianapolis, Ind./Cambridge, Mass., Hackett, 1995.

5 Ibid., p. 347.

6 Ibid., p. 348.

7 Ibid., p. 356.

8 Ibid., p. 355.

9 Ibid., p. 357.

10 Ibid., p. 347.

11 Moritz Schlick, 'On the Meaning of Life', in *Philosophical Papers*, ed. H. Mulder and F.B. van de Velde-Schlick, Dordrecht, Reidel, 1979, pp. 112–129.

12 Ibid., p. 114.

13 Ibid., p. 113.

14 'Nor can we find any action in human life that is not directed to some other end, with the exception of speculative consideration. For even playful actions, which seem to be done without any purpose, have some end due to them, namely that the mind may be relaxed, and that thereby we may afterwards become more fit for studious occupations; or otherwise we should always have to be playing, if play were desirable for its own sake, and this is unreasonable.' St Thomas Aquinas, *Summa Contra Gentiles*, in *The Basic Writings of Saint Thomas Aquinas*, Vol. II, ed. Anton C. Pegis, New York, Random House, 1945, p. 45.

15 Ibid., p. 60.

16 Ibid., p. 55.

17 Albert Camus, *The Myth of Sisyphus and Other Essays*, trans. Justin O'Brien, New York, Knopf, 1955, pp. 12–13.

18 Richard Hare, 'Nothing Matters', in his *Applications of Moral Philosophy*, London, Macmillan, 1972, p. 33.

19 Ibid., p. 38.
20 Ibid., p. 35.
21 Albert Camus, *The Stranger*, trans. Matthew Ward, New York, Knopf, 1988, pp. 120–121.
22 Hare, 'Nothing Matters', p. 36.
23 Ibid.
24 Robert Bolt, *A Man for All Seasons*, New York, Random House, 1960, p. 8.
25 New King James version, Ecclesiastes Ch. 1, verses 3–4.
26 Ibid., Ch. 2, verse 17.
27 Ibid., Ch. 3, verses 11–12.

Reading

W.F.R. Hardie, *Aristotle's Ethical Theory*, Oxford, Oxford University Press, 1968.

*E.D. Klemke, ed., *The Meaning of Life*, Oxford, Oxford University Press, 1981.

Thomas Nagel, *What Does It All Mean? A Very Short Introduction to Philosophy*, Oxford, Oxford University Press, 1987.

Steven Sanders and David R. Cheney, *The Meaning of Life: Questions, Answers, Analysis*, Englewood Cliffs, N.J., Prentice Hall, 1980.

David Wiggins, 'Truth, Invention and the Meaning of Life', in his *Needs, Values, and Truth*, Oxford, Blackwell, 1991.

Jonathan Westphal and Carl Levenson, eds, *Life and Death*, Indianapolis, Ind./Cambridge, Mass., Hackett, 1993.

Index